Reviews

Lee Sannella must certainly be, in the realm of Consciousness Studies, a national treasure, period! He has been everywhere, talked to everyone, practiced with everyone, and thought hard and long about what is real and valuable. This remarkable summary of his decades' long Odyssey will surely remain a classic.

Seymour Boorstein, M.D.,
Associate Clinical Professor of Psychiatry,
UCSF, School of Medicine

About two hundred years ago William Blake and Beethoven were contemporaries: and both of these incomparable artists equated God with Genius. Lee Sannella, my dear friend of forty years, today has expanded this joyful news into his study of genius in the language of today; an achievement itself of genius, extolling the glory of practicing one's own unique gifts, whether they be very high or modestly low.

Duncan Bazemore, Ph.D.
Professor Emeritus, Religious Studies
California State University,
Humboldt Arcata, Calif.

Lee Sannella takes us on a magical mystery tour through the world of mystics, psychics, and healers, revealing astonishing events in remarkably clear, straightforward prose. A fascinating book.

George Leonard, Aikado Grand Master,
author of *Mastery and the Ultimate Athlete,*
and *Education and Ecstasy..*

Lee Sannella has been a pioneer in bringing to the attention of Mental Health professionals the so-called Kundalini awakening phenomenon, a profound spiritual opening many gifted people undergo. Kundalini experiences often mistakenly (and sometimes with tragic consequences) have been treated as a form of mental illness. In his memoir, On Genius, Sannella tells us of his many fascinating excursions into the realms of higher consciousness. He brings us with him on his journey, enabling the reader to meet many of the geniuses of our era who have not received the recognition and appreciation they deserve. Sannella has given us vivid first-hand portraits of these special people which are not now available elsewhere, and which we may never see again.

John E, Mack, M.D.,
Professor of Psychiatry,
Harvard Medical School
Pulitzer Prize-winning author

On Genius

An Evolutionary Force
Inherent in Every Being

Lee Sannella,
Eye Surgeon
and
Psychiatrist

Copyright © 2006 by Lee Sannella

ISBN 978-0-7414-3456-2

Cover photo & design by *Soos Works*, Islesford, ME
A Lee/Joan Project

Published by:

INFINITY
PUBLISHING.COM

1094 New DeHaven Street, Suite 100
West Conshohocken, PA 19428-2713
Info@buybooksontheweb.com
www.buybooksontheweb.com
Toll-free (877) BUY BOOK
Local Phone (610) 941-9999
Fax (610) 941-9959

Printed in the United States of America
Published June 2013

In memory of my mother Susan,
and my father Salvatore

Acknowledgments

The first book I wrote was privately published in 1976 and went through several printings. It dealt with kundalini and proved a satisfying experience, bringing to the fore a much-needed awareness and understanding of this neglected subject. Over a period of about twenty-four years it sold fifty thousand copies and became a minor classic in the field. However, it took twenty-seven years or so before I started more writing. This time the subject matter was about the experiences of various talented people, and I felt it would make the book I wanted.

Friends who love me, and whom I love, rallied and helped me develop the courage and confidence I needed to bring this vision of mine to fruition. I think particularly of Roy Dixon, JoAnne Sunshine, Chris Tong, Anne Howell, Trish, and Georg and Woody Anderson. They were friends who held my hand when indicated or knocked me on the head when necessary.

Happily I had Anne Howell nearby, keeping me centered and helping me vent my emotions as I struggled. JoAnne Sunshine had the unenviable task of clarifying my almost-undecipherable pages of longhand and getting them into the computer. Professional formatting was done by Karla Andersdatter. A major crisis was averted (saving me a goodly sum of money, time and grief) by my sister Joan's daughter Susie who rescued the manuscript in Quark and converted it to Microsoft Word. After this, Joan together with her invaluable friend and computer operator, Mark Goodman, were able to diligently proofread and edit the final manuscript.

Each and every one was an essential part of the work and together, in the best of Gestalt processes, made the whole greater than the sum of its parts. These friends were an inspiration and support without which my hopes would never have been realized. They made it a great trip. My appreciation knew no bounds.

However, much to my dismay it seemed that the ink had barely dried before dissatisfaction set in. As I reviewed my work, the glow I expected was not there. I struggled with this dilemma and realized I had more to write.

It became a long and arduous task, much longer and more arduous than I could have imagined. Where would I have been without my sister Joan and her computer friend Mark, who together worked indefatigably, Joan experiencing along with me times of near-exhaustion. Again, my loyal friend Anne stood by and thwarted the slings and arrows of outrageous fortune which strewed my path. She rescued me over a hard patch with her computer, as Wayne also did with his. All have my undying thanks.

I have been blessed all my life with wonderful people whose love and encouragement have added so much to my life and therefore to this book. (I will not be surprised if some of you recognize yourselves here.)

I love you all.

Foreword

I first met Dr. Lee Sannella is 1982, and today feel privileged to count him among my friends. Our initial contact occurred because he had authored *The Kundalini Experience,* a breakthrough contribution to a widely misunderstood spiritual phenomenon that has long intrigued me. Ever since that time, I have valued him as a fellow investigator into the psychospiritual dimension of human life, and also as a fellow traveler on the path of self-transcendence.

Throughout this span of over two decades, I have known Lee Sannella to be a fearless champion of the creative, visionary minority—men and women of his own ilk. In his book *On Genius,* he recollects some of his fascinating encounters with truly inspired and highly gifted folk, who fanned his own quest for self-understanding and, in some ways, brought him closer to the edge of spiritual creativity, where things either fall apart of fall into place.

On Genius is a priceless snapshot of an entire era marked by the so-called "counter-culture," exposing largely its hidden underbelly where seminal ideas were spawned...and often ignored and forgotten. With the fine eye of a retired psychiatrist—and I should add, the precision of an ex-ophthalmologist—Lee Sannella reveals the human side of his subjects, and in doing so lacks neither the necessary tolerance nor liberating humor.

As is evident from his whole approach, we must count him among those he would consider as having found their passion and will to exercise their heart's desire. May this book prove a catalyst for those who are still reluctant to embrace their genius and an enjoyable confirmation for those who do.

Georg Feuerstein, Ph.D
Author of *Lucid Waking, Holy Madnesss, The Deeper Dimension of Yoga,* and *In Search of the Cradle of Civilization*

There is a vitality, a life-force, an energy, a quickening that is translated through you into action, and because there is only one of you in all of time, this expression is unique. And if you block it, it will never exist through any other medium and it will be lost. The world will not have it. It is not your business to determine how good it is, nor how valuable, nor how it compares with other expressions. It is your business to keep it yours clearly and directly, to keep the channel open.

Martha Graham

Author's Preface

Rereading my manuscript and feeling dissatisfied was a disturbing and conflicting experience for even thought I had completed the work, yet the work was not complete. I remember the first question I asked myself was, *Why* did I write it?" When the answer surfaced, it seemed that I did so to examine the question, *Of what does genius consist?*

I became consumed with a need to write more on this subject. My mind had been aroused and with a mind of its own went galloping off, expanding extravagantly as it went. For concentrated months I read, pondered, entertained constant bursts of thought, discussed them, wrote and rewrote. Ultimately, like a movie of an explosion run in reverse, the little and big pieces of ideas flying off into space began to retreat as fast as they had advanced and finally coalesced into a more or less tidy center.

I came to see that genius is a Divine gift, a capacity however large or small, which all people have at birth. It is a process of finding your passion, mind, will and determination to exercise your heart's desire. Not fulfilling it will deprive you of much of the joy of living. Genius is fragile and if not responded to will not come again.

Many times a simple explanation to those I work with has seemed to strike a chord "that sounds like a great amen." Both they and I know there is much more to divulge, so I plumb my own depths and theirs to constantly clarify greater, deeper truths that may emerge, often delighting but also leaving us facing harsh truths.

Here are stories about some of the cosmic explorers I have met personally or through their writings. These geniuses will be introduced through my star-struck eyes.

Outstanding visionaries, they followed their passion single-mindedly. This is what drove them through extraordinary experiences which also led them to a greater understanding of themselves and the nature of existence. But their primary efforts always was to express their genius, sometimes to communicate but not to indoctrinate.

As you will see, my fascination is with the visionary essence of genius. That has been the perspective which has evoked the most meaning and is the source of the excitement which adorns and renders holy all my life.

My writing about them has helped serve me to honor these great ones, remember them and bring them to the attention of my readers before they are lost forever. I invite you to a feast of genius, the remarkable force which drives humankind ever on and up, even to the everlasting source of all and all.

Chapters

Comment

With the understanding that genius is the spark of passion found in each of us, a natural birthright, the thought comes that we need to know how far back in the history of the development of modern Man can we see evidence of this passion. Fortunately, Lyall Watson has written a fascinating book, *Lightningbird*, which follows the emergence of genius, starting over a million years ago.

Lightningbird

One Man's Journey into Africa

Christopher Bird, one of my dearest friends, a genius, now dead, told me of Lyall Watson's *Lightningbird*, Christopher's words were, "...this book proves once again that the few mavericks [geniuses] among us are capable of revealing more new truths than a horde of mandarins."

Reading Watson's book is an electrifying experience. He tells the story of Adrian Boshier's solitary treks deep into the African bush where he collected the information and artifacts essential for Raymond Dart's research. Watson writes so beautifully and fleshes out Boshier's journey in such a masterful way that you find yourself breathlessly hanging onto the graphically-written stories of Boshier's adventures, some of them life-threatening. You keep in step with him as he gains knowledge, discovers tribal secrets, and partakes of tribal rituals.

Here is where we learn about our beginnings. Watson reminds us that Africa was our cradle where we were born and lived in small numbers about five million years ago! In a gorge 300 feet deep in Serengeti were uncovered three kinds of hominoids who lived 1.5 million ago. By about a million years ago Africa and parts of Europe and Asia were peopled by a new breed. They, like all the others who went before them, had to meet the demands of the ongoing radical changes of climate and environment. However, they unlike the others, were vigorous and inventive, glowing with the first sparks of true Creativity. They were geniuses as much above their ordinary contemporary humanoids as our geniuses are beyond us.

Boshier's collections indicated the paths these geniuses took as they slowly progressed through the ages, bringing us to where we are today. In the beginning, they used their hands but then one or more of the inventive ones used more than hands. These individuals effected simple extensions of their arms by reaching for what was available nearby to help them do this. What they found and used were long bones, clublike bones, horns with sharp points which could puncture and mandibles with a few teeth which could be used as saws. Their use was naturally copied by others and became widely used. These were their first tools and were produced by the geniuses of their time.

As life progressed, other geniuses turned up as they always do. They did more than select tools for a necessary need for survival. They had chosen needs which could not be satisfied by found bones. They had to work on objects they found, bending them to meet their chosen needs. In doing this they made the enormous conceptual leap from tool-using to *tool-making,* another act of genius. This was a giant step in human evolution.

Eventually they used more than bone, teeth and horn. Geniuses helped usher in the Stone Age, remarkable for its creativity, Watson presents mind-blowing examples of early civilization (as we measure it today) among these ancient peoples.

Campsite floors were littered with objects we call artifacts or tools. In all caves were found bruised pebbles called "hammer" stones. Those early geniuses figured out how to "carve" harder stones by the "hammer" stone's property of breaking—loosening—the bonds that bind harder stones together. Also found were chopper stones.

Stone was also used to make hand axes. The stamp of genius was clearly on them. These were classic oval forms crafted in elegant style and design. They were the first undeniable tools showing real evidence of creativity or in my word, "genius." In this mental leap our Dartians became truly human.

Unbelievably, Boshier found stones so perfect (without flaws and cracks) that they rang when struck. Some of these stones had dents and grooves indicating where they could be struck to ring. They are called gong stones. In Viet Nam there is a stone-age "lithophone" altered by man that is tuned to sound intervals of a 5th and a second and third harmonics. In South Africa are similar stones—one of these was a six-foot boulder which was split horizontally and became warped so that the upper part is supported by the lower in only a few places. Hitting the upper portion at man-made dents produces a note in G, B-flat and C, the 6th and 7th and 8th partials of a lower tone 2 octaves below middle C. Only the geniuses of those ancient peoples could have effected these results.

Only a human can select a stone and use it as he likes. These ritual scars can be very articulate and indicate the unbelievable transition from instinct to intelligence, found only in man, and made by the geniuses of that time. Still used in the early twentieth century, talking drums are a long-used innovation as an example of a truly evolutionary progression, impossible or improbable as a random event.

The hand of genius is seen everywhere. Art is rampant. The Makaberg living in the high mountains have wrought paintings in caves two million years old. Some show how a bow can produce a musical note. Some cave paintings, found far below the surface of the earth, exhibit extraordinary beauty. Lavishly reproduced in photographs, they are the equal to the finest paintings of today and are accepted as having been created by geniuses. Cave paintings have been called the archives of the oral history of Africa.

Still more evidences of creative genius in manual and intellectual skills have been unearthed. In Swaziland were found *40,000-year-old* precursors of writing (the first sort of hieroglyphics) and math similar to artifacts found in Europe, 20,000 years later. Other archeological findings have produced a wealth of data going back hundreds of thousands of years on mining and demonstrating specialized uses of precious stones and gems.

Our nascent prehistory of the mind indicates the origins of worshipful peoples as seen in two million-year-old paintings. There are insights about death, birth and the sacred. The stars and extraterrestrial realms were being noticed. The Dogon's geniuses knew that the star Sirius had a dark "brother" before our astronomers proved it.

Artifacts, which Boshier collected, were essential in proving that modern man's birthplace was Africa. Perhaps more importantly, they gave evidence of the progressing genius from the earliest hominoids and marked the path that genius took in the evolution of human consciousness.

Reading about the prehistory of Africa's hidden keys, many of which have now been uncovered, is an illuminating experience. These keys revealed the first leaps by geniuses in the evolution of mind which gradually led to the first sparks, the first dawnings of consciousness, of genius, the only evolutionary force *continuously available* through a divine spark. Genius may be propagated only by this spark, by separate acts and progressions which by my definition will never occur again.

The earliest progress made must have taken millennia and the work of thousands of geniuses who lived in that first culture of bone, tooth and horn, well before the Stone Age. Imagine then, how long the Stone Age took and the stages of development beyond that. Each of these noted "evolutionary thrusts" progressed by the constant acts of genius. Each magnificent addition was made by acts of genius, propagated only by this divine spark, which is the only gift with man as its provider.

It should be noted here that there is another very important view of Man's origin as eloquently put forth by Lawler. His book is titled, *Voices of the First Day*, and is a detailed revelation of the case for Man's origin in Tasmania. But whether in Africa or Tasmania, this evolving of mind is miraculous to those who recognize it, even as others see nothing. We ask ourselves, how can it be that there has been so much evidence found of early man's genius and our inheritance of it, and so little note taken of it in our twenty-

5

first century. We are here to acknowledge and bow reverently before the passion of those geniuses who have brought us to this point. We must bow before the message that each of us is endowed with the gift of that divine spark, however small, and our progress depends upon its being acted on. The imperative now for us is to recognize it and use it wisely.

Comment

Fewer and fewer of the more primitive cultures have been able to maintain their way, but traces of their heritages can be found.

Aboriginals

The remnants of several great cultures have been virtually eliminated by the encroachment of our modern, Western barbarism. In America, Australia, South Africa and in scattered pockets elsewhere, these folk were the primal, basic, absolute visionaries.

With their loss, our term "visionary" has become shattered, fractured into uncountable shreds and fragments that disturb our Western dreams as if to remind us of a golden age now gone where we once had a connection to the cosmic domain and all of nature. They practiced no warfare, no self-flagellation and related aberrations. They 'just was'.

Pomos and Elsie Parrish

In the early 60's, a group of Quakers I was involved with were invited to help some local Pomos construct a new teepee, build a foot drum, repair the roundhouse and build tables for a picnic area. I went out to the coast with my wife Tresa, our four kids and some friends of the children. The Pomo tribe of a few hundred was located off the coast about 80 miles north of Santa Rosa.

We ended up working alongside Pomos of all ages. In the midst of all this, I was able to have many conversations with Elsie Parrish, a powerful woman and the chief of the tribe. She told me about a pow-wow or celebration that she went to when she was about five. There were several young bucks who were looking for support in their bid to become the next chief. The most prominent of these was a high stepping braggart and showman who was in fine fettle giving speeches and compliments and strutting around promising to serve them all well.

Little Elsie was a friend of the old chief and the two of them were wandering hand in hand some distance behind this young showoff noticing his antics and something else. Elsie and her old friend were seeing something quite invisible to all but the two of them. They glanced at one another to assure themselves that they were both seeing the same thing and burst into gales of derisive as well as full-bodied laughter.

Unnoticed by all of the other guests was an imp of a being who, or rather, which, was imitating every move and cry of the performing Pomo. The little one gave an exaggerated performance, poking fun at the young man for those who had eyes to see at another dimensional level. Naturally, only those so talented could partake in this farce which was a serious matter as well. For one of the eligibility requirements for high office in the tribe was the ability to see and hear on this subtle level. Training in many other subtle skills was also required. The two of them had a great laugh at the expense of the young brave and thus Elsie was brought to a greater understanding about what was involved in the leadership of their people. This was her first initiation, to be followed by many others. She was trained for high office throughout her life and her leadership role was gradually assumed as her skills increased.

Elsie explained to me what was involved in her role. According to their customs there were four offices or functions which optimally would be filled by someone for a lifetime. In fact, Elsie had finally been given the offices of Great Dreamer, Medicine, and Prophecy. She never assumed the fourth office of Miracle Worker, though we had heard that she had frequently drawn fire down from the roundhouse roof or ceiling during healing ceremonies in her adolescent years. She was apparently able to handle that position as well as the other three, but for her own reasons, did not choose to do so.

The Great Dreamer function seemed to be crucial for the survival of the tribe in the midst of the encroaching and uncaring, and sometimes even hostile, white world. The great dreams she would have throughout her life indicated changes the tribe would be well advised to undertake. These varied from negotiations and trading with their neighbors, both white and Indian, to changes in spiritual procedures, alterations in full dress costumes, dances, which tribal stories to use and when, and all sorts of practical day to day things. The office of Prophecy seemed to not be as well defined, but, these prophecies were listened to with great care, and Elsie and her many helpers interpreted them.

The prophecies gave them all great hope and a feeling of understanding in the midst of the many pressures and uncertainties of their tribal lives. All of this contributed to greater intimacy, love, respect and cooperation. The role of the shaman and the trance dance, the Making of Medicine and miracles dominated the tribal life of most North American Indians, as well as aboriginals worldwide.

Elsie had been afflicted by diabetes early in her life and I heard that she died not too long after we were with her. There are pockets of Pomos all over Northern California becoming more and more contaminated by our exploitative Western monetary ideas. Arguments over gambling rights promise to sow more discord than wealth among these beset Americans. At the time I was there, they were getting ready to set up some gambling concessions and seemed to be going ahead without any real planning. The power struggles and divisiveness between tribes were disappointing to see. It seemed to me that their venture would have benefited from a more cooperative spirit

Yurok Indians of the Klamath River and Delta Bay/Harry Roberts

I was introduced to the Yurok culture through our children's piano teacher, one of the few left who would come to our home to give lessons, in about 1952. Alice would tell us stories about her husband, Harry Roberts and thus, we were gradually introduced to him. He was a remarkable and interesting man. This was his second or third marriage, but the only one Harry carried on about was his first love as a young man when he was being reared by the Yuroks. Harry's life with them had started as a boy when he and his family moved to the mouth of the Klamath river where there was a salmon processing plant. Harry's father was in charge of that operation which was located in the center of the salmon dominated waters and inhabited by the Yurok Indians.

As a boy, Harry was completely captivated by this remarkable tribal civilization. He spent most of his time with them and with his teacher, Robert Spot, who, in effect, adopted him. Robert Spot was the last full chief of the Yuroks and he presented Harry with a series of tests which were necessary to prepare him for the role of tribal leadership. The first challenge was to be able to hear "the rock" speak.

One summer I went with Harry to that very same rock, which he pointed out to me there on the beach at the Klamath River Delta. I approached the rock with more than a little caution and consternation. What might take place? Would I hear something or would I draw a blank?

So there I am with my ear plastered to the rock, wondering what I am listening to, or for. After a time I realized that something very subtle had been going on for some time now and then it began to make some sort of sense to me. I was hearing a sound which was more like music than a voice—subtle, so that I had to really listen.

It was like the way you would have to "look" if you were trying to tune into an elf or nature spirit a la Robert Ogalvie Cromby. That is, one does not "look" straight on but sort of obliquely. So it was with this listening. One could not dissect it, or use one's faculty of discrimination at all directly, but only perceive this "out of the corner" of one's mind. Elfin fairy "voices" do not easily yield their secrets any more than they yield their forms to the tribal people in Elsie's gathering. Only she and the chief could see the derisive elf and all of its antics. So while I got only the hint of a whisper of these fairy sounds that day, it was memorable enough to be with me as I write today. Thus I received the merest hint of what it must have been like for Harry in his boyhood being guided by the great Robert Spot through test after test.

I recall Harry looking at me with his sly, critical, demanding, piercing and glittering eye as he said, "You know the Yurok child is taught but one lesson at a time. If the child or young person cannot answer the question his teacher asks, then he simply goes off and "studies" that area until he comes up with a better answer. Until he does, he is not asked another question. His education has come to an end until one thing at a time is mastered."

So Harry's lessons went from the simple and mundane to the heights of the secret teachings held in reverence by the tribal elders and chiefs. "The rock" was first, and later there were more difficult trials. there were tests to see if you could talk to the fish in the bay to see which were ready to be caught. Harry's first giant step in the tests of manhood was the making of Medicines.

This "maha" test was the test of water or the ordeal of the sea. The aspirant was required to swim out to a large rock which stood at least a half mile out in the bay at the mouth of the sacred Klamath. Then he was to circle it and hit it with his hand on the far side before returning. The strong currents make this is a very difficult undertaking and so this was called," making one's water medicine".

Following this was the making of the land medicine. For this he arose in the dark of the night and dressed in only his drawstring and his medicine pouch, he would run full tilt through the forest listening for the telepathic instructions of his teacher who followed, always keeping a half day behind. At the crack of dawn, Harry had not fallen down and broken a leg, run into a tree or similarly disabled himself.

Then, as a part of this same trip, the spirit medicine is made. Harry continued to run for three nights before the spirit trial started. His teacher directed him to find a cave and to spend the night there in chanting and prayer, making a medicine packet from the materials in the pouch he had brought. Then he was directed to find a ledge in the cave and to feel for the packets of medicine left there by candidates who had endured this very trial at some time in the past.

Harry tells it this way: "I find this cave and I do my medicine thing—then I reach up to put it on the shelf and, just out of curiosity, I run my hand back and forth to feel and know what's there. I feel a crumbly packet and another, hardly a bundle at all, and then only dust with a few lumps, so I get the hell out of there. It's a sacred and spooky place. I spend the day as directed and later, just for the hell of it, I go back and look for the cave. I couldn't find it. I must have made a wrong turn but I couldn't find it. Even the ones I did find did not have any shelf. I couldn't understand it. Soon Robert shows up and greets me in ceremonial fashion and I know from the twinkle in his eye that I made it and I dance around for Joy. On the way back I asked about the cave and Robert said "You say you couldn't find it?" "Yes, there's no place like it". And he laughed himself silly and I saw he knew it all and then I saw it all as well and I said "you mean...???" And Robert shouted: "YES! YES!" and we both roared our joy to each other."

Even though the Pomos and the Yuroks have different cultures, there are similarities in how they recognize and cultivate the talents of a candidate who might become their next shaman. Such care and discrimination, or in our terms, hierarchical distinctions, are carried to great lengths all over the tribal world.

In the Tibetan tradition, the practice of divination directs their priests to discover the Tulku, or lineage holder of their unbroken spiritual line, and makes this continuity possible. Succession by virtue of blood line alone, which is now practiced by the regimes of royalty throughout the world, seems to be a degraded version of these anciently cultivated virtues.

Robert Spot was willing to see Harry become the next chief—even though he was an Irishman with red hair and only a trace of Indian blood, because he had demonstrated that he had the talents which were required. His observed and acknowledged qualifications superseded the fact that he was not even a tribal member. That is true hierarchy. But it just wasn't to be. Harry was not able to make a clear choice. He was a man divided in every respect—by his language and his blood. He was drawn more by the world of possibilities than by the role of chief of his newly adopted tribe.

The Yurok culture had in place perhaps the most distinctive, astonishing and complex societal structure that one could conceive of. Harry described it to me over the years until he died in the 80's. To my knowledge these things are not revealed in the scholarly literature, or in Erikson's work. Even Krober—the great UC anthropologist did not write about these things. And it is even rare to hear about it in their oral tradition.

Harry was certainly grossly prejudiced in favor of the Yuroks, but this did not diminish his reliability as a reporter. The Indians always knew that their most loyal and fiercely idealistic supporters were white people who had become "converted" to the Indian's way of life. So, they were always on the lookout for such souls. Harry was certainly one of these dedicated enthusiasts.

I don't believe he was ever caught in an inconsistency and his certainty seemed not to be affected by his addictive tendencies—very prominent in his Irish heredity. He was addicted in the best and worst ways to alcohol and tobacco, and he told great love stories. His love for his adopted brothers, the Yurok was unshakable. And his anger with the white culture for their unconscionable treatment of this fast dying dream world of native Americans was fierce.

When drunk, Harry would look at me and pronounce "You're OK for a white man, but really none of you are worth a damn!" Then he would lapse into semi-coma and carry on long monologues in the Yurok language, waxing eloquent with tears falling down his troubled face, mourning the decline of himself and his dear departed brothers and sisters.

Drunk or sober, Harry loved to tell me of his people. One day he reached into his shirt, and my breath whooshed out of me at what I saw. Suspended on a cord was a nearly round stone the size of a small chicken egg and speckled like a piece of smooth, polished granite. Most remarkable of all was the way it was held by the string. There had been a hole drilled through it and it was strung from this. Harry said: "This is a dinosaur crop stone (indicating that the Yurok had known for centuries that these beasts were birds) and it has been handed down and worn by our chiefs for untold ages. The last guess that all the experts who had seen and examined it was that it was at least 25,000 years old. When this stone is in constant use it holds great power to heal and prophecy. But when such an object is not used by a shaman as an intimate part of his work of magic and power, it loses its mana." He would then dismiss it as a 'has been' saying, "Oh it doesn't have much force now." Harry would say this, just as I would say genius not followed will perish through non use.

Once he said, "You know we are the only ocean-going Indians in America. Just look at the design of our canoes with the high prow—obviously made for rough water. We have legends of trading regularly with the people across the Pacific."

Harry also kept two day and night baskets, about 2 inches wide. And he had a pipe inlaid with mother of pearl which was passed from person to person, promoting harmony. He showed me a few other interesting objects— wooden hooks for netting fish, and some sewing tools.

Ten years after I borrowed and photographed these things, the crop stone disappeared. I thought it would be interesting to have these objects "read" by someone who was a good psychometrist (where the reader holds such an object in his hand and then gives you a verbal impression of the pictures, incidents, thoughts and voices which are perceived in such circumstances of focused attention.)

I still had these things when Peter Hurkos, world renowned Dutch Jewish psychic was being tested by Charles Tart. It was obvious that the testing situation was interfering with any talents Peter had, and this is not unusual when dealing with the combination of science and the subtle. However, when Peter and I sat alone while I transcribed his words, he was able to offer beautiful cameos which suggested where these objects had come from, who had used them and which described the essence of something quite wonderful and elusive that these objects transmitted.

When I presented these impressions to Harry he was amazed and happy to have some confirmation about what he knew of their history.

One of the most puzzling and absorbing of Harry's legacies, about which Harry could carry on endlessly, was the mystery of the Yurok language or, rather, languages.

The Yurok used two languages, the one that everyone used, and the one that was used in private circumstances. He referred to the latter as "the high language".

There were two distinctions in their society: the high and the common, which he even called the "low" people. And it went further. Harry actually described the skin coloring as lighter in the high. He said that many of the

High among them had lighter hair, blue eyes and sometimes reddish hair and were more slender in build.

Many times Harry would (mostly when drunk) speak in one language and then translate this into the high language, pointing out to me that the latter sounded more like Gaelic than the common base from which most of the Indian languages were derived in the Americas. He didn't describe any difficulties among the tribal members resulting from their social position, office, or intermarriage. It's a shame that none of this was recorded in Harry's time here. He occasionally referred to certain cultural and physiognomic aspects in greater detail than the ones I can remember here.

The "low" people were stereotypically described by Harry in terms which I am sure would be offensive to the surviving Yuroks today. But Harry never expressed any prejudice nor stereotypes in referring to black people, Chinese or Japanese despite the sort of gross descriptions he used to describe the Asiatic features of the Yurok Indian culture. He always stoutly maintained that the "low" people were not deprived in terms of treatment or rank on tribal councils which was accorded to them based on talent, expertise and training. The genetic diversity of these two lines was maintained in the old days. But this changed rapidly over the 60 year span of Harry's life that was spent with them.

I believe Harry's first love and wife was Yurok. He described her as a light haired, carefree beauty whose loss he was still mourning now forty years later (in the 70's). As Harry's death approached, he gradually spent less energy on dwelling in the land of their high language and began to spend much of his time in his "mothers presence" singing all the little boy songs he knew to any and all who would listen, in English. You see, Harry had lost Robert Spot quite early in his life—about the same time his father died, but his mother was very much alive on my several visits to her home in the 60's.

He spoke most eloquently of the Yurok's connubial arrangements. Each couple had its own place in the surrounding forest which they usually went to for intimate and sexual occasions. And there was no lack of adultery. It seemed to be a topic of good natured humor and even glee among the children who were constantly spying on their elders and bringing their affairs to the "public" eye.

The vast Yurok territory was preserved by a highly developed system of responsible stewardship. There were specialists in every aspect of hunting, fishing and land management. Each activity had its own intricate system of guidelines. Those whose specialty was the Deer culture would be responsible to "call" the deer and would assist the hunters in tracking—but he would NEVER KILL A DEER HIMSELF.

He was then given his own portion of the kill. And in the fishing culture, there were similar customs that were honored by all. Harry said that the display of special talents was expected; it was even acceptable to brag about one's prowess, but exaggeration was never tolerated.

Harry was one of our last Renaissance men. He wrote fluently, was expert in goldsmithing, and photography, he was a designer, botanist, nursery man, and naturalist. He easily won all the prizes at the county fairs for native Californian exhibits of plants, and above all he was a great and humorous story teller.

He wrote a lengthy treatise on horticulture but his benefactor at the Green Gulch Zen Center, where Harry spent his last few years, and where he died, never published it. It was full of the most exquisite illustrations and photos and it included, I am sure, Harry's 500 year plan for the Zen Center.

I assisted the residents in carrying out the initial plans for moving and planting salt water resistant trees in a grove close to the ocean. He included instructions about where and when each planting should be made and why. Even when Harry was in his decline he told us where to go and collect these saplings and how to plant them which we did with great holiday spirit one week-end or two. Harry was a great visionary, replete with his own faults and weaknesses, but still living and dying a warrior priest. I once asked him to show me where the amanita muscaria mushrooms were and perhaps the more rare pantherinas.

Harry answered, "Yes, yes, you'll find them 600 feet off shore under the Bishop pines."

So, together we sallied forth for the north coast and the pines and there they were in great profusion. We picked a trunk load of them. I don't remember what I did with them except for drying and tasting a few, very delicious, but I didn't take enough to experience their hallucinogenic effect. I must have given them away, as I habitually did with all of my most prized possessions.

As he lay dying he asked Herb Arnold and myself to get a mess of salmon, the king variety, not silversides, and he tried to give us detailed directions for their smoking. He told us how to build the smoker and to gather alder wood for the fires. We did all of this as an act of love and respect for Harry. And I trust that by now Harry has reincarnated in one of his beloved Yurok villages to take up the leadership for which he was so lovingly groomed, and which he did not choose in this life.

Comment

We have geniuses whose passions have not been encumbered, interfered with or threatened by the powers that be. These are the geniuses whose expressions chanced to be acceptable to their society, or at least not considered important enough to be a threat. Their passions could flow unimpeded.

Markham

By my definition, great genius is the extreme example of any lesser, self-styled genius. In order to highlight this process, I used the more extreme examples. But it is important to stress that under this definition, everyone has the potential for genius, however small, and exercising this potential thus expresses our latent species essence.

Once our genius is revealed to us, we seem to share certain characteristics. We have a secret view of our own rectitude, and we pursue it relentlessly with whole-hearted concentration. In fact, we engage this process as we would a religious, revelatory rite, offering this singularity as a prayer, as a contract with whatever happened to cause this revelation. We focus our energy toward our creative process and express it in our real world or other lives and/or symbolically. But regardless of our methods, we actively pursue our calling to the extreme of our capability.

We illustrate that this contract is our focus, duty and joy. We work toward doing it supremely well. Actually, it is our answer to the demand of The Divine, a demand which would not, could not ever be made again.

One's response is always unique and the only suitable answer to the Divine Source. No one else can ever do it as we envision it, and this clearly delineates that it is one of a kind. Whether a flash-in-the-pan or a life's labor, it is itself alone and never possible of duplication, just as one's fingerprints are unique, never to exist in precisely the same pattern again. Even failure is part of this process; no other person could possibly understand what its "is-ness" is, or its "was-ness" was.

Often heard are ignorant and dismissive statements such as, "Oh, in the great course of time, Tesla's 'secrets' and Mozart's music would occur." No, No! This is not possible. Genius itself is what God is about and such God-given marvels will never happen again in just this way.

Oprah Winfrey's magazine recently carried an article in which was written that passion and talent is the essence of what is truly Great. With all due respect, what we speak of here is in a totally different dimension. The Great Ones were Divinely endowed and had no way of understanding what was going on with them. Thus, they all died inviolate and pure.

Just as I was trying to get this notion across to my lady, she insisted I run it by my friends to test its reality so I met my two confidants. For several hours we discussed it and then looked for a location where we could talk further without interruption. We finally found a quiet place in the local library. It had been set aside for music and we had not known of its existence before. As we sat and spoke, gradually we became aware of a violin on the couch against the wall. It drew us up in wonder. We were fascinated by its extraordinary trim, its glowing appearance and subtleties of finish.

A man came into the room. He said his name was Markham. He said he was a finisher of violins and the owner of this extraordinary instrument. He explained that it had been fashioned and finished by his own hand. What was remarkable was his telling us that he found with each stage of his work, the quality of tone became increasingly more beautiful, in fact incomparable. He had created this work over years, and he was the sole manifestation of it.

I asked him as he spoke, would he give this to the world. He answered oh, no, not at all—ever! Here we were, transfixed at this epic moment, and he was announcing that this perfect instrument was the end-all of his existence.

He was inviolate just as all my recorded geniuses were, knowing for sure that their particular talents were unique and in no manner could be duplicated. Hearing this pure assurance of this creator, we were totally convinced of the rectitude of what we had been discussing in theory, and we were struck dumb as we saw the theory before our eyes suddenly becoming transformed into living reality. We were offered a gift, as if from a super-divine god. Only a creator of such a marvel knows his own child immediately and without qualification of any kind, and this is his gift from that Divine source within himself.

Think of the ninety-nine percent of us privileged earthlings who have not realized, and may never realize, this precious birthright of that Divine source however small it may be. Doing what you love and refusing to compromise (compromising is detrimental) is your gift from the Divine, your inherent spirituality and the meaning that you follow as your guide in life. If it doesn't have meaning, it's too early or too late for you. Think of your own worth in these terms and resolve to pay any price towards its discovery and awaken thus to your own incalculable gift and the necessity for you to hone this process perfectly.

Peter

Since writing this, I have had several interviews with a dear friend of mine for twenty-five years, Peter.

When he was fifteen years old, Peter was asked to perform Beethoven's First Piano Concerto with the Los Angeles Philharmonic Symphony. Due to his increasing workload of studies to enter the medical profession and later with the responsibilities of family life, he virtually dropped his musical career.

Circa 1998, he reinitiated his piano practice on his Roland digital piano. By attaching headphones to the piano, he was once again able to intensely immerse himself in the study of classical piano literature.

Currently, he delights in honing his performance 4-12 hours a day, bringing his art to ultimate perfection. He has gone into exquisite detail in this development of his virtuosity, especially in detailed descriptions on the art of pedal usage—innovations hitherto unknown even to the greatest virtuosi! He has created enough of these innovations to write a manual which would be useful for students in their advance stages of development. He is also composing a piece based on Dickens' *A Tale of Two Cities*.

If my hypothesis on the uniqueness of genius is accurate, it is unlikely that anyone will ever be able to recreate Peter's insights. Therefore only he can write about this fruit of his art.

His critical and incisive remarks on other virtuosi have no parallel in the realm of professional critique. The same is true of his insights and performance of Chopin's compositions. This talent alone could make Peter the greatest appreciator of Chopin ever.

Peter's sensitivity to his craft is evident in this recent (slightly edited) letter to me:

Dear Lee,

Enclosed is a summary of my thoughts on the piano, as I discussed with you. The piano is a pliable instrument, but only when it is allowed to use its own true character. This can never be done by an attack of force—or pure technical prowess. Thoughtless repetition will only enforce an already poor approach, which would make the piano sound like a drum.

The aim of the pianist would be to produce a bell-like tone, which sounds after he key is struck—ever under the pianist's control. This enables the performer to merge the sounds as he will—either with the following notes—or all alone—and control the tone in the manner of a violin or a voice.

Before I describe some techniques to accomplish this process, let me digress and describe the piano's unique character.

Whenever a key is touched, a hammer is released. This sets up an aftermath of overtones, harmonics, and oscillations. These interact with the strings, the sounding board, and the rest of the piano. This is where a musician can take advantage of the sonorous after-sounds—the resonance—in order to modify, to amplify, to harmonize, and to make the music flow naturally—all under the pianist's control.

Most importantly—never make any muscular effort. Use only the weight of your arms, hands, fingers, and wrists. The hands, and especially the wrists, must be in constant motion—rolling, sliding, and rotating—all without effort, controlled only by their own momentum.

On difficult passages—or even easy ones—the fingers, the wrists, and the hands are to be positioned so they literally fall into place. I admit this is opposite to what is usually done, but the effort is rewarding. It makes for beautiful music—as well as fewer injuries to the fingers and

26

*the hands. I compare this with the Zen Buddhist approach—
to go with the flow—and yet be in control.*

*As an example, a rapid series of octaves or chords
should be played with the wrists as fulcrums, allowing the
weight of the hands and arms to create their own
movement—your force on the first chords should be enough
to carry through all the way to the finish—like ripples on a
pond.*

*Now as to the fundamentalists: each key should be
played with a staccato approach but controlling the release
as needed. This approach gives the musician the advantage
of keeping the tone in place, and an opportunity to
manipulate the pedal to evoke and control additional
changes in resonance.*

*I believe the pedal should be employed—by being
introduced only after the key has been struck. This serves to
take advantage of the piano's natural harmonic—then
release when ready for a pause or break.*

*When to introduce the pedal, when to release? Here I
am at a loss for words. Of course we've all been taught: "a
change in harmony requires a change in pedal"—but that
leaves all musical instruction aside.*

*The music must be your guide. The underlying
harmonics—must be sought for guidance. Feel. Listen.
You'll find it.*

*A note aside: each piano has its own character, its
own sonority. What may be correct for a light-actioned,
bright piano might be far different in a mellow heavier-
actioned one.*

*I hope my ideas might be of some help. The piano is
unlimited—it has every capability of the voice, the violin,
even more!*

*For effective practice, one needs to produce each
tone as bell-like as possible. With this in mind, unnecessary
repetitions will be avoided, and practice will become a joy.*

*Yours truly,
Peter*

This is the profile of a piano Zen Master. Optimally, he will, in person and by book, instruct a new generation of geniuses. I weep with joy, feeling his task in its borning (*inception?*). Will he ever donate this majesty to those of us who hunger and thirst for it? Who can tell.

After a long time of silence, I had the impulse and phoned Peter even though I had been told by his friends that he had not been answering the telephone for two years. To my surprise and joy, Peter answered the phone himself, and this now is a new chapter in our relationship which promises much.

Erik Erikson

I once asked Harry and some of those who knew Erikson, the specialist who came to study the Yurok and wrote of them in *Childhood and Society,* what they really thought of him. Fanny Fish, the Yurok tribal healer was not reticent, but used a minimum of words to describe her summary view of that scholar and wonderful man.

She said, "He has brains like worms." Now these are Harry's words, not mine, or necessarily hers.

When I finally met Erik Erikson, a delightful scholar and his beautiful wife in their home through my friend Herb Arnold, I approached him about the Yurok's reception of him. He laughed and laughed and told me this story:

"I was in the foliage doing research and I was so preoccupied with this that nightfall came upon me rather suddenly and then I had to consider where I was to sleep. After all, their place is miles from any kind of public accommodation. So I asked one of the men if they had any place for overnight guests and he acted sort of shocked and said "Oh no, no place, no place at all."

And we talked a bit more and he seemed to hesitate, to reconsider and then he sort of mumbled that "there's the church, but no", he added, "that would never do. It's no place for a man to sleep—full of pews and what not, no, no place. "

And then I broke in and said, "Oh that's fine, I can make a small space there for my bag and mat. " But then my unwitting companion in this effort said, "He wants to sleep in the church. That's no place to go." "But," I cried, "There is no place else to go." "Oh well," he replied, "I guess you can try, but really, it's no place to sleep."

So off I went on my sleeping venture, into the old church—an innocent surrounding. A place to sleep. So I settled down for the night, I thought. About two or three hours later my slumbers were disturbed by a fury of rustling noises which sounded like Niagara Falls. The whole place, and especially me, was infested by flying things, bats, going about their night feeding. And maybe I would be their next target. I was already dodging the little monsters. "This really is no place to sleep!"

And we both laughed. I was relieved to learn, to my surprise, that the antipathy which I had always felt in struggling with the heavy, almost Germanic style of this great author and gentleman was simply because I had expected him to be an American, or at least British. To my embarrassment and chagrin, he was really a Teutonic scholar and there was no way that this man, the epitome of Thomas Mann, could write in a trenchant American manner. So, I became his ally once I understood. Would that it could always be so simple to be magically converted to intimacy with every soul we met.

Walter Russell, 1871-1963

Walter Russell was a multi-talented genius, a musician, writer, painter and sculptor. He was the author of a book titled, *The Message of the Divine Iliad.* Always unbelievably physically healthy, he said in all his life he <u>never</u> felt fatigue.

All of his creations brought a response of enthusiastic acceptance and national recognition. The statuaries were amazing. Huge groups were assembled, one being Mark Twain surrounded by his characters. Busts of some of our presidents are unbelievably lifelike. All of his works were recognizable and beautifully presented. But more than that, they all fit in with what our country valued, symbolic along the lines of "motherhood," "apple pie," and "the flag." He never had to buck the current and didn't find it difficult to be successful , to come upon the scene in great strides with an over-abundance of energy and drive. And he didn't see why anyone should not be able to do the same.

He gave a talk in 1946 which was made into a small book with the title, *Genius is Inherent in Everyone.* The quotation on the cover of this book is as follows:

Mediocrity is self-inflicted;
Genius is self-bestowed.
The Choice is yours.

He is included in this book because of his philosophy of genius. He is also a perfect example of the easy road a genius would have if, by such a rare occurrence, his genius was complementary to the country he lived in. Unfortunately, non-threatening genius is usually an oxymoron

Carl Ulrich Schnabel

My musical life was always given a lot of attention. Sometimes that took the form of attention to the fact that I was totally ignoring music. This began to be painfully true as I started to lose my hearing when I was about 75. For many years before that, I had been the most faithful follower of a great musical figure. I had been going to his yearly appearances at the music Department of Mills College in Oakland. He was the son of a giant in the musical world—internationally very well known Arturo Schnabel, pianist extraordinaire. This idol of mine was Arturo's son, Carl Ulrich Schnabel.

He was an absolute joy to see and hear. He did master classes on the stage at Mills for an audience of several hundred, mostly students of the piano. Carl was a superb performer and an unequaled teacher on the level of a Gattegno and, in addition was as loving a human being as I have ever met. He poured energy and love on each student and all of us present. He evoked the best from each student and the best in attention and regard from everyone in his audience as witnesses of every nuance in each masterpiece on stage. He gave freely of himself as a performer, even his mere asides he threw at us with abandon and great verve. And as a stage presence he was perfection itself, so full of humor and good spirits that the most stage struck of his students were able to respond to this profound ambiance with their best—even more than they had been capable of the instant before. I was so upset when I heard that no professional recordings were made of these great lessons. And how much more would have been added by good videos as well. Which reminds me of my sorrow at not being able to arrange for Julio Silva, the professor at the religious school in San Rafael, to record his essence teachings of Gregorian Chants of which he was said to be the last real expert alive.

For years I had studied music privately and then by correspondence with the Music Department at the University of California in Berkeley—first counterpoint then later harmony. Then came that dear old man, Professor Silva Julio (whose son was first cello in the New York Philharmonic) and for whom Julio wrote a concerto. It was he who helped me notate my original compositions—the lyrics and melodies I wrote for my love-struck states (the exception was De la Mare—"The Horseman.") I had already done the music in my head but had never formally written it down as I was very inept at this. Nor was my piano playing up to what I could imagine it should be. So I had to have help and his was masterful and consummately loving throughout. The man was such a love. I never was able to get anyone to put these on tape and so hear them full with a fine singer but this could be done later for pay, as they say.

Andreija Puharich/Uri Geller

At first, I knew Andreija indirectly only through rumors. He worked part time at Kaiser Hospital in Oakland as a Neurologist/Internist for a few years before I was appointed to their eye department. He had already left by the time I started with them on a full-time basis.

I finally met him at June Degnan's and her psychic brother in law, Michael's, regular soirees. She was "Mrs. Well-off", a Democrat and an early spiritual seeker. Michael was an avid reader of Jung and things psychic and was a very literate and skilled psychic reader of us all. We stuffed our heads with Michael's glamorous little gratuities for several years. These embraced the whole spectrum, from miracles to mysterious aliens. Andreija had already been globetrotting in psychic circles and with high-tech physics folks when money through friends and small funding sources came his way.

My impression of Andreija in a nutshell: he always went for the cream of any subject and didn't mind spilling a bit of milk. He never forgot his roots in Yugoslavia. It marked him somehow in all his ways. Charming raconteur, researcher of the obscure and miraculous without parallel, he was a good friend who was easily affronted. Sensitive and with a kind of pride, he was never the great Guru figure of his inner dreams. He was full of ambition and always very mysterious. He created his complex karma, almost as if it had been intentional. But I also saw that he had a very loving heart. He was a good father and a dear friend. He wanted to be very famous and super rich, and he never became either by his own standards. This again is the common denominator in most of the geniuses I have known who are in the high-tech fields. Such an attitude leads to personal tragedy in more cases than not.

The one major fear he suffered was that of his keen mind becoming old or useless or betraying him in madness. He could take almost anything but this, and yet paradoxically, he easily surrendered to experiments, totally leaving his intellect behind. I never discussed this with him at sufficient length to get to the core of it—other than this insatiable curiosity of the unknown which I so admired in these visionary geniuses.

A friend, knowing Puharich's attraction to experiments and his insatiable curiosity, felt that he, Puharich, would be drawn to the remarkable Israeli psychic, Uri Geller. Geller had built a reputation by displaying his considerable psychic talents on television and live theater performances. What was more intriguing to Puharich was that Geller needed help in the research he had set up to study his own psychic powers. Not unexpectedly, Andreija, our golden boy, took up the challenge and flew to Geller's rescue, and they ended up working together for several years studying Geller's psychic abilities.

Puharich and Geller left Israel and came to the U.S. They continued their research in Puharich's laboratory in Ossining, New York, and Geller continued to entertain by demonstrating his unusual abilities to eager audiences. He would bend spoons without using any physical force. He would do demonstrations on TV where the audience was invited to put their out-of-commission watches on the stage. Uri would then get many of the watches to start spontaneously which garnered him a lot of publicity. Puharich ultimately convinced Geller that his future didn't lie in show business and that his psychic talents could be put to more interesting uses. During their work all sorts of paranormal disturbances were reported.

I heard that Uri once stopped a cable car while it was rolling down the mountain and then restarted it again, the cable car operators never guessing the real reason for its temporary interruption.

Again, when Uri was displeased with some personal arrangements he had made with Puharich, he apparently teleported Puharich's large Mercedes Benz out to a nearby swamp. They had to call the fire department to get the car out, and the firemen were totally baffled because there weren't any tire tracks on the muddy ground anywhere in the vicinity.

Another time, Uri said he was walking down a street in New York, distraught about some family matter and was wishing very ardently to be back in Ossining. He suddenly disappeared from the street and the next event he was aware of was crashing through the panes of glass of the gazebo in Puharich's back yard.

At Stanford Research Institute, Uri got in big trouble. He and some of the rest of us frequently visited Hal Putoff and Russell Targ there, observing and performing PSI experiments with their team and a clairvoyant. When Uri was there, which was quite frequently, all the computers at times, and lab instruments as well, would go berserk and behave in most bizarre ways. Even the magnetometer there would go off on a spree. This angered and upset the resident physicists and government sponsored projects no end.

One day, as the three of us were walking on the beach in San Francisco, a most unusual thing happened. We approached a nearby restaurant for lunch and entered the place, pausing a moment at the door. A waiter pointed out a table for us and we chatted away, slowly approaching the table. Geller cried out: "Look Lee, Look Andreija!! See that fork" (as he pointed to it a couple of yards away) "it's already bending." And sure enough the fork had started to bend. One of its prongs was bent at right angles and it continued to bend as the three of us stood there watching it. None of us had touched the table yet. We sat down and Uri said to me; "You are good for me. Things can happen much easier when I have that kind of energy around me."

Andreija, our action arm and always ready to leave home visited Arigo, the greatest of the Brazilian espiritistas (healers). Arigo's miracles were performed with an ordinary worn pocket knife with the assistance of "Dr. Fritz," a disembodied spirit who worked through him. His patients experienced no pain, no bleeding, and the surgical wounds closed themselves without scarring immediately after the procedure.

Arigo was already well known in the psychic world through John Fuller's book, *Arigo: Surgeon of the Rusty Knife*. Arigo died, as he had predicted, in an auto accident. After he died, for some reason, the authorities wanted to view the remains. They discovered that a complete autopsy had already been performed with no one's permission. Since his death, many Brazilian healers have surfaced, claiming to be channels receiving Dr. Fritz's assistance.

The best authority on channels I know is Lama Segyu Choepel Rinpoche. He is a spiritista healer and is now the founding director and head Lama of the Healing Buddha Foundation, a Tibetan Buddhist healing lineage. He told me that only three of those channels were probably authentic channels.

Adreija, listed as Henry K. Puharich, M.D. wrote in the afterword of John Fuller's book: *"I want to present a personal interpretation of what Arigo means to me. To understand that, one has to have a feeling for what it must have been like to be "inside" of Arigo. Let's begin at an elementary level, namely, the feel of Arigo's hand while doing surgery.*

"If you take an ordinary butter knife and gently run the edge across your skin, you get an idea how this knife feels in the hand that moves it. You will notice that there is a gradation of pressure that can be applied, and that applying this pressure gives you a feeling of frictional forces, resistance of the tissues to being cut, control of the movement of the knife, and so on.

"You could learn all these nuances of the feel of a sharp knife by maneuvering it over other materials, such as foods used in your kitchen. In short, you would learn what every surgeon learns—the feel in one's hand of a knife against tissue.

"Now I thoroughly knew this feel of a knife in my hand when it was used in surgery—human or animal. One day when I was standing beside Arigo in his Congonhas clinic, he asked a patient to stand against the wall—a man of forty-five years. Altimiro, Arigo's assistant, handed a sharp, stainless-steel kitchen knife with a four-inch blade to Arigo. Arigo grabbed my right hand, thrust the knife into it, and closed his hand around my hand, so that the knife was doubly enclosed. Then he led my right hand toward the eyeball of the patient and ordered me to put the knife in the eye socket. I followed his orders and plunged the knife between the eyeball of the patient and the upper lid. As I did so, my right hand went limp—I could not proceed. I feared that I would slash the eyeball and do permanent damage. Arigo again grabbed my right hand and said, "Go ahead. Do it like a man!"

"This order gave me the courage I needed. My fears vanished, as I plunged the knife deeply into the eye socket. Now I was in complete control of myself. As I moved the knife into the depths of the eye socket, I was amazed to discover that the tip of the knife had none of the familiar feel that a knife has against tissue.

"To give you the complete feeling of what my hand felt, do the following exercise: Take a pair of magnets and find the like poles of each. Then hold one magnet in each hand and bring the like poles toward each other. You will now experience repulsive forces between the two like magnetic poles, and these will be felt in your hands. This is a totally different sensation from that which you experienced with the butter knife against your skin.

"Now when I moved the knife into the tissues of the eyeball and the eye socket, I felt a repulsive force between the tissues and the knife. No matter how hard I pressed in, there was an equal and opposite force acting on my knife to prevent it from touching the tissues. This repulsive force was the secret of why no one felt pain when Arigo did his famous "eye checkup." My patient did not feel any pain from my knife manipulations either.

"It is obvious to me that Arigo could control that repulsive force so that he could go ahead and cut tissue. And this, of course, should cause pain. But it is known that Arigo did not cause pain. I have observed, and so have others, that Arigo could cut tissues without using the sharp edge of a knife.

"Often he would cut using the dull edge of the knife. He has been known, when in a hurry, to cut tissues without a knife. In these rare instances he would use his hands and fingers to go through tissue. It is my opinion that the actual cutting agency was the repulsive force, and not the knife or his fingers.

"I have no idea as to the nature of his repulsive force. But from electrical field measurements I carried out on Arigo (EEG, EKG, and GSR), I do not believe that this repulsive force is in the electromagnetic spectrum. I believe it is an unknown form of life energy."

Andreija and I once went on a search for Pachita, miracle healer of Mexico City, finally locating her in the city after several hours of driving. The room she was working in was very dark. She was bending over a small boy who had an egg-sized tumor on his scalp. Pachita took up a large hunting knife and cut out the growth. The child protested loudly and we could tell that he was really hurting. Andreija had similar rough treatment with the same knife stuck first in one ear and then the other with much pain. One of the attending Americans there asked me: "What is that peculiar smell?" and I muttered: "They are shitting in their pants from pain." Pachita was losing her power to do crude surgeries without pain and would soon die. All the well-trained healers could easily accomplish this, but this siddhi was gradually lost in their declining years. My MD friend and partner, GC had been to Pachita earlier when she had complete control of pain and regularly performed miracle surgeries.

I was able to make several trips to Mexico with Andreija. The most outstanding figure for me was the curator of Archeology at the Institute in Mexico City, Von Vertanau, who had spent his life "proving the genetic strains out of which emerged our modern Mexican." This determined scientist had dug up hundreds of clay figurines in his ardent pursuit of his own Mexican origins. These statuettes were of three types: those with great scimitar-like noses which were easily identified as being of Semitic origins, Negroes with the typical African mien replete with huge thick lips, and Orientals with their typical pigtails and epicanthal eyelids. What self-respecting Mexican would want to be rudely awakened from his romantic dreams of descent from Spanish dons and dark-eyed senoritas?

I spent many happy hours with this brilliant man and his many figurines, while Andreija searched for his version of the Holy Grail. In the process, he left even his good friends "at home" while he pursued his many more glamorous associates and his strange peoples and places in and around Mexico City and Teputsland. He chose to go out and visit these strange folk who had seen some weird lights and God-knows-what rather than go into an archeological museum and see a very interesting scientist at work. That didn't interest him very much.

Andreija went forth to conquer, making quick and easy friendships with such notables as the Hawaiian Kahuna, Daddy Bray, who earlier attended some of our soirees at June's place, and many similar folk. He found one pal after another all over the world, and he promised much but rarely stayed long enough to deliver. Thus he made many acquaintances and created a miscellany of disappointed collaborators. He had a real life replete with house and several great sons and daughters. But he was well known for his affinity with talented and beautiful psychic women and had a fantasy of quite an other-worldly empire well in place. He called it Spectra and continued with his interest in it peopled with its strange folk, mostly brought to him by a weird succession of psychic readers who channeled these friends and "family" of a dream world he knew through their and his combined eyes and psyches.

Freda Morris and I spent many exciting hours in his Ossining NY home working with one psychic reader after the other. All were women, most of them young. I met Freda at a conference in Cupertino in 1971. She had taught hypnosis to medical students at UCLA School of Medicine for some time. We were immediately attracted and the next few years were filled with a wonderful exchange in which I returned to the study of hypnosis and Freda studied music with me. We toured the British Isles, visiting all the notable psychics we could meet using Freda's charm and intuition, which she possessed in abundance.

The Ossining, NY trip was part of this many-year odyssey concerned largely with the psychic world and its fascinating folk. Freda wrote many books on hypnosis and together we wrote a magazine article on our adventure with a South San Francisco Poltergeist.

This all started one evening when I was meeting with Lou Bostwick and a group of amateur psychics at his Berkeley home. Suddenly, at the hour of ten, when no good Berkeleyite would think of phoning, as everyone who is anyone has already started for home, this jangling, startling call came out of nowhere and a screeching, hysterical voice was audible to everyone at the meeting.

"We are in trouble. Come immediately to help us. Help!! Help!!" was the pleading, but not very intelligible call. After more of this they calmed down a bit and they gave us a brief account of the awful things that were happening in this beset and beleaguered family from Daly City and South San Francisco. Like a voice out of a dense fog, they entreated Lou, whom they had heard about over the psychic grapevine, to help them.

It was a Latino extended family who had, a year or so earlier, been intruded upon by their young daughter's marriage to a Jewish man. She was pregnant now and expecting soon. Things in their home had started happening spontaneously—water all over the floor, books falling off the shelves, silverware flying off the table, and then, horror of horrors, fires breaking out in the back rooms with no one nearby. People were rushing in to put the fires out screaming and there were general hysterical outbursts. And this was not all. At times they had to put all their knives out in the washing machine, in their garage. But to no avail. These same knives might at any time float into a room and hurl themselves into the wall and fall to the floor. Well! This was too good a fair to ignore! We all crowded into a big Mercedes and took off like gang busters for their home, forty minutes away.

On arriving, they first insisted that we go to the dwelling they had recently abandoned due to all these abominations. So at their insistence we all went over to the abandoned place. Just as we drove up to it, one of us saw a woman's white face in an upstairs window and then it disappeared. So we were suitably spooked even as we entered this place where from the disarray Old Nick himself may have been expected to appear any second.

Putting on our best front, as investigators entering a battlefield, we strode into the building. Some idea of the scale of this situation could be gauged by simply looking around: water on the floor, burned curtains, books all over— general pandemonium had reigned here for some time. As we milled around, Lou exclaimed "Look! Things are different at this end of the room." And, indeed, as the group divided, there was a distinct difference in the apparent heights of the people on one side as compared to the other. "It's a vortex", Lou said. And the hair on my neck rose as a chill ran over my spine. I gulped and wondered what fantasia would be next.

Well, we trooped upstairs to see and it was an unholy mess. Things were scattered everywhere. I set about arranging everything in a definite, easy to remember, orderly pattern and we returned to the lower floor. We were quite silent now, so when a loud banging from upstairs began, it was easily heard by all.

We rushed upstairs again and there was the horrid mess—recreated. We all took off. We had seen enough to know that the family's flight from there was totally understandable. We visited these quarters many times during the next year. Once the old grandmother was choked by a pillow over her face as she was walking in the house and had to be hospitalized. The young couple once went shopping in San Jose, forty miles away, and their car keys disappeared, only to turn up in their house that same day. And a fire had started in the crib of the baby, now safely born. I was there and was slightly burned on one hand when I rushed into the room to put it out.

On one occasion, when we were standing by, the mother went to diaper the baby and she found (and we saw) a chain with a crucifix wound around his genitals. We did not witness the weird instance when an egg flew by, broke against the window and egg ran down the inside AND DOWN THE OUTSIDE of the intact pane of glass.

One visit by a local psychic of no small fame was very funny. He came in with his usual self assurance and sat down on the bed and proclaimed: *"I dare you to come out and show yourself!"* Immediately a knife flew across the room. He turned white and jumped up and fled the premises, never to return.

Priest exorcists visited and, though things got better, they did not cease. But wonder-of-wonders, all of it ended when the Jewish son-in-law decided to become converted to the charismatic Catholic Pentecostal sect that his wife's family had joined years earlier!

These startling and dramatic events are all within the domain of Poltergeists, or noisy ghosts. We are forced to posit the existence of so-called "lower-entities," to bring some meaning to our overwhelmed senses and sense of reality in the face of such distortions that defy ordinary logic. (Remember Jung's description of noises coming from a table in his home in his Memories, Dreams and Reflections?)

I am reminded here of Geller and the unbelievable things which happened in his presence. But many times, these anecdotal stories carry a kind of verification of the more subtle laws governing the astral realm that, at first glance, seem like nonsense. Geller had valuable watches break, precious gems fracture, and banks of computers cease to function in his presence. This is mostly in the category of psychokinesis or PK. It is an hypothesis of mine that the neurological disturbance known as epilepsy can partially, or in total, be caused by an internal disturbance in the homeostasis of the brain, which can cause massive electrical discharges or epilepsy.

This is suggested by the cessation of epilepsy in Brazilian psychiatric patients who began to study to become trance mediums. I followed the medical histories of five epilepsy patients who began to study with Lou Bostwick at his Psychic Institute in Berkeley and I saw a comparable diminution of epileptic seizures.

The indications were that learning to conduct the tremendous amount of psychic energy, which had piled up from nonuse within their nervous systems, had a favorable impact, lessening the frequency of their seizures. Similarly, in the case of the young Jewish father whose family was beleaguered by the poltergeist, his frustrated spiritual equilibrium, and the upset of his family's spiritual equilibrium may have precipitated all of those phenomena, because once this religious issue was settled, they disappeared.

Geller had a similar excess of psychic force operating in him, and it was almost totally uncontrolled by him. Once he found another outlet, such as the healing experiments he had started when I was still seeing him regularly, he may have been helped to control these aberrant psychic forces. The power of the psyche is even better attested to in the case of Chi masters. Certainly some of them, just as the Philippine healers, as part of their training, were able to set fires by mental means alone.

Joyce P, a coal baron's wife, lived with Andreija for some time with her talented psychic children and the children that she and Andreija shared. They lived on the huge and beautiful one hundred square mile retreat called Devotion that the Reynolds family had created in North Carolina.

Sharon was one of the channels I met while she was working with Puharich. They had an interesting tiff once, when Andreija was reluctant to share the limelight with her on some esoteric physics paper he did. She claimed that it all came from her channeling. They were both right. Over the course of five years we had a lot of meetings with Sharon and her friends. Then something strange occurred one night when she and a friend presented us with a paper that he had done on the alien craft landing in New Mexico. After that she just disappeared; I never saw her again. Arthur Young (inventor of the Bell helicopter and author of *The Reflexive Universe*) called her the greatest psychic he had ever worked with. He couldn't resist the charm and beauty of this quick witted intuitive psychic reader.

Through Andreija, I met Adam Trombly. He was in as desperate a need for funding as Andreija, and so found his way with me to a week of drinking and good fellowship with the only true philanthropist I had ever met, Josh Reynolds, III. He had supplied Andreija with a beautiful home and laboratory there, at Devotion near Dobson, North Carolina. Andreija ended up feeling betrayed when he saw his financier reaching into his deep pockets for Adam.

And then, Andreija invited a melange of old and new friends he had hoped would supply money for him, and they opted instead to support the most vocal and attractive group there—the whale watchers. Again, instead of Andreija! Andreija was very upset and our brief weekend ended. So we all left Devotion. I didn't have any contact with him again until I phoned him upon hearing of his illness, and we had a touching and wrenching reunion on the phone, promising each other that we would meet for Thanksgiving, which was only a few weeks off. But it was never to be. The next morning Andreija was dead. Sic transit gloria mundi.

Robert deRopp/
George Ivanovich Gurdjieff

Robert deRopp is the author of *Drugs and the Mind*, which was very widely known in the 70's as "the druggies handbook". In the early '60's, after an interesting meeting with this distinguished writer, scientist and student of Madame Ouspensky (of the Gurdjieff circle of teachers) I agreed to help him form a Gurdjieff study-work group. Our first meetings were well attended and were held in an abandoned spiritual center in the Berkeley Hills. When Robert had culled this motley gathering of curiosity freeloaders, he transferred his operation to his ranch and center on Sonoma Mountain. Over the next several decades (sometimes weekly and, at times, with months of inactivity) there gathered around him several hundred "seekers" who came and went, as was the case in all new age spiritual groups, whatever their merit.

Perhaps the best that can be said of this experiment was that it encouraged Robert to write several fine books on various aspects of his project. In the end, Robert judged the whole show hardly worth the price of admission and shuffled off to better worlds. Still in his youngish, old-age prime, well preserved, witty and philosophical, skeptical and intensely practicing his own disciplines including a skillful OOB existence, at its best one of the most fitting keys to the other kingdom, and at its worst, at least an effective instrument to nullify the usual terror of death and dying.

Work with him convinced me of the genius of Gurdjieff as dancing master and inspired leader/teacher of his students. But, altogether, the limitations in Robert's students seemed due to the same obstacle in Robert—he did not demonstrate a fully and truly open heart.

I met deRopp casually, years before I became fascinated with his preoccupation with incarnating the work of Gurdjieff which had been adapted by Ouspensky and his wife. His training in biochemistry and related disciplines enabled him to make as much income as he needed to acquire several acres and buildings on Sonoma Mountain.

Robert did not welcome any attachments to himself that might lead to becoming personally dependent on him. He was a remarkably talented critic of all he surveyed and he also was a gardener, artist and a fine writer. He must have written a half dozen non-fictions on everything from science through politics of community to religion. Most of them had been well received—especially his very timely *Drugs and the Mind.*

He enjoyed and suffered a difficult marriage to a sensitive and creative woman who staggered under the burden of the label "schizophrenic." He had children from an earlier marriage and there was a young son from this union.

I remember well my introduction to his activities. It was like walking into an Alice In Wonderland world of artists and artisans. And I was amazed by the community that was recreated each weekend, becoming invisible during the week. Sundays, in accordance with the best Gurdjieffian custom, were spent in strenuous work, their traditional and beautiful movements, with all aboard becoming quite drunk as the day wore on.

Robert was especially jovial and friendly and even emotionally confessed if one read his body language and didn't listen too carefully to his caustic commentary—which he never lacked.

But when drunk, he came across as one big joke even as he initiated a long conversational stream enjoyed by all. Those occasions are, even now, strangely haunting to me. They hearken back to the flavor, rather missing in America, of a relaxed European elite who knew too much and were proud of it.

The Gurdjieff movement, despite Bennet's efforts to enliven and perpetuate it, never did take off here. The branches that survived illustrated the many fantasies of "would be" Gurdjieffians, each in their own manner. But few contained much heart. The head managed to call the shots despite the various body disciplines that were added by the many aspiring little gurus. And indeed, it was this limitation that I suffered more and more consciously.

Rumors circulated of a meeting, in the wee hours of a weekend morning, in a meeting hall none of us had ever heard of. And tales of a great Gurdjieff Guru circulated in the right channels. I remember all of us waiting for the master's triumphant, nonchalant oozing into the room and how he began a conversation he never stopped during all of the years that I knew him.

Once we had a place above a bar in San Francisco. I had been drinking a beer there and passing a few words with an intelligent, perceptive gent when this little guru walked by us and the same gent turned to me and said: "I know that man. I was with him in New York. He's a consummate actor and con man. His great weakness is his hatred of women and, besides that, he's an enemy of every man." This remark fell on well-prepared ground, as I had noted these flaws for some time and had decided to ignore them for the rather bleak, after many repetitions, virtues I was enjoying.

Soon after this incident, I left all of this neo-Gurdjieffian stuff behind me. I had an awakening in which I walked out of a meeting and never came back. This sort of reflex decision was typical of me. I would put up with a lot of nonsense, out of a perceived sense of loyalty and inertia. And then suddenly I would leave, as is more typical of a woman who puts up with a marriage and then is suddenly gone, never to be heard from again. But in this story of my often blundering, heavy-footed thumpings through the miasma of a New Ager's searchings, much had to be endured before a powerful search light would turn itself on to illumine a more adequate way for me.

It's late enough now for me to round off the deRopp story—a poignant ending in the long hard battle that his life was. In one of his last books, Robert propagated a vision of community based on the eternal truths of religious prophets' lives. He wrote *Church Of The Earth*, and in retrospect this was more a cry of pain, as is every great vision in the face of this mundane, earth-based, power and money oriented society, which is now consuming the planet in a paean of greed.

Robert found rest in his hero's ending, his own obituary—his last book. And surprisingly enough, it was in this magnum opus that I first became acquainted with what his true spiritual discipline and life-long practice had been. For obscure reasons of my own, I had never asked him the questions about himself, which might have led to his having had more of an influence upon me.

For all his adult years, first learned at Madame Ouspensky's competent feet, he had been practicing OOB (out of body travel). Ironically, it was soon after those very early years of the sixties with Robert, that I worked with another Robert (Monroe) in his first seminars on OOB.

I believed at that time that this was an effective way to cope with the ever-present fear of death and dying and to better understand the after-death states. Other practices in Islam, Christianity, Hinduism seem similar in nature.

They might have the effect of altering our state to a more open and primal vision, but in OOB there was a consistency of experience and result that I hadn't found elsewhere. Years later, the kundalini experience became my focus, but even then, practitioners' claims about managing their fear were never as convincing to me. And, all the extra drama—enjoyed and suffered—didn't help. It was never convincing to me as a clinician and experimental scientist. If there was one thing that I wanted more (at that time) than God Realization, it was to conquer my own fear of death.

Spiritual disciplines seem more and more to be a process of surrender to a Guru, living or dead. They amount to a real opening to life and death, at all times. Disciplines are rather useless for their own sake. I recall a conversation with

Baker Roshi and Brother David Steindl-Rast in which Baker Roshi was holding forth on the virtues of Soto meditation; and Brother David, after these observations, which were all old hat to him, remarked to Baker: "You might find much virtue in metal bending and fire walking, too."

Very true, for those practices seemed to necessitate the sort of surrender I felt I needed; feats of surrender which were verified by gross, physical 'miracles'.

But now I come to the parting of the way with the Gurdjieff disciplines. I think in my case, more hazards I no longer needed to subject my already sufficiently punished old body to, and could walk away from.

Many of my friends had been successful in Zen ,and I, still not much distanced from a certain over-dramatization, idealization and macho, said to myself: "Oh hell, what am I doing in this mess". And I turned to my Gurdjieff friends and said: "Thank you. I'm leaving you." And I never saw either of them again.

I joined the L.A. Rinzai of Maesumi Roshi, a bright young Japanese teacher who had received Inca from both Soto and Rinzai Zen masters, to whom two of my friends had gone recently with some real success stories to tell. This meant that I would fly all over the state where I could, like the Buddha, sit until I wore my backside out—determined to do this until something happened.

And that's what I did for four months, suffering through numerous, weekly seshins. So there I was, in my fourth seshin, grinding away like a workaholic on "Mu!". By tradition, when a monk asks the Buddha: "Does a dog have Buddha nature?" Buddha answered with a familiar enigmatic syllable of the day: "Mu!" So Roshi and I were blasting away at "Mu!", counting our breaths and periodically asking to be struck on the shoulder muscles near the neck. The sergeant at arms carried a big stick and usually only struck those who requested it—to keep one awake or shocked back onto the track.

Maesumi quite readily displayed his short-tempered response when students did not drop in to be guided two or three times a day during the long seshins and especially when they showed no signs of progress. Hindus specialize in long meditations with little body movement, while Zen practice is more compassionate and only required thirty-minute sessions with walking meditation in between. Occasionally, after a bellow from the Roshi, the Sarge would pass down the line and strike everyone, whether they asked for it or not—an effective attention-getter which promoted intensity in our sitting.

On the second day of a four-day seshin, feeling like I was going nowhere slowly, I went in to the Roshi and began to bellow Mu! —not, I'm sure, convincing anyone of my seriousness. But suddenly the Roshi leaned over to me and said: "You pass." I was really astonished at his expletive and my response was immediately negative. What do you mean I pass? I passed nothing. I'm nowhere. What are you talking about?

"But what will your friends think, Lee?" the teacher said.

That one stopped me. The next day, same story. But, upon sitting with the Roshi and being asked a simple Dharma question, I was dumbfounded to hear myself mumble some obvious nonsense, way off the track.

Roshi exploded: "You know better than that."

I shouted back: "Of course I do, but you're driving me crazy."

He retorted: "Oh, go back and sit down!"

So out in the Zendo, there I am huffing and puffing again when suddenly everything changed. I became struck dumb and terrified. I was experiencing total chaos of mind. Thoughts tumbled and plagued me. I bit the bullet and stuck to my no-motion state of petrification, mental and physical, for what seemed like hours of abject torture, and then a blinding thought completely silenced all the chaos. Two words penetrated my entire being: 'God Is!'

I burst into tears and danced in place with joy; completely blissful, humbled and for the first time in my life, completely in one piece and in a place of no separation from all and everything. I wanted to jump up and seek out my enemies and shake them and say: "I love you. What a fool I've been to judge who you are without clear recognition of and certainty of the existence of the Divine."

How can anyone become truly responsible for his or her actions, thoughts and all the insanities of one's separate ego self? 'God Is' meant that I am in God and that force is in me forever. Despite my doubts in the past and those to surely come in the future, I would never again be totally alone without the resource of KNOWING.

And there was nothing of personality in that source. It was simply inherent, contained in all the substance of the cosmos. Not personal in its caring for each of us, it was caring itself, embodying all the virtues in, and of, all of its manifestations.

This was the answer to the central question of my fifty years of pain and frantic seeking. Always before my question had been: does God, does this force, really exist? So, for thirty minutes I bathed in this bliss of knowing and utter contentment.

It faded, of course, but two days later, back at the job, I had the impulse to take a bus to work where I usually biked. As I approached the bus stop, the world began to seem utterly transformed. My psyche was aroused to a feverish pitch as I got on the bus. I sensed the bus talking to the driver, and as the bus started the bus spoke to the road through its tires. And as people got off and on, I studied each one and instantly knew their inner thoughts, their mood and all about their lives. This persisted for four hours during which I saw patients in this gift of ecstasy. Of course, it all faded and my first half day of ecstasy was gone. (Almost, never to return.)

Maesumi was very helpful, in retrospect, as a kindly authority figure. Not so much a model of Divinity who could transmit this essence to me, he seemed to know how to reinforce my own innate ability.

Maurice Rowdon

I met Maurice Rowdon in Berkeley in about 1980 and worked with him in his version of Reichian breathing. His adopted device, or work to survive here, hardly represented much of what he was: a historian, talented critic of Renaissance art and music and visionary aspects of animal intelligence and who knows what else. Rowdon's book, *The Silver Age of Venice* contains some fine writing about Renaissance Italy's art, music and culture. He once owned and managed a vineyard in Italy and made his own wine years before. However, he became disillusioned by the declining qualities engendered by the mechanization of the wine making process. He came here to the US only to become similarly disappointed.

He became very involved with the subject of communication with animals and their trainers. Not surprising, the trainers mentioned here are women. Women have special talents. Most channels are women. Women are more competent and intuitive with animals than men are. They demonstrate a heightened sensitivity to, or intimacy with, non-human life. Penelope Smith is an inter-species telepathic communicator who communicated with whales and other oceanic mammals, and wrote *Animal Talk*, (Beyond Words Publishing Co., 1999).

Rowdon, in his travels, discovered a German woman, Hulda Heilmaier, who practiced the dark arts, Black Magic. She also had trained two German racing dogs in language, math and communication using front paw-to-hand signals. Maurice was with her for several months before writing his book titled, *Elke and Belam,** (Random) about these fascinating animals. These dogs demonstrated to me the quality of non-human intelligence—which is every bit as remarkable as our own, but in unexpected ways.

Maurice and I had for some time promised ourselves the adventure of going to the Palo Alto hills to view Coco, a wonderful chimpanzee and her trainer, Eve Anderson. We were fascinated by the interaction of these two beings. I had a brief, loving encounter with Coco, who had been trained to develop apparent talents in sign language. This dear chimp turned to her small audience of Maurice Rowdon and her trainer, and in sign described me as 'the man with a hole in his hair' (my bald spot). Coco's charming trainer had difficulty understanding this chimp's intelligence in terms other than that of a retarded human infant who would offer others the most delicious grass and flowers. Rowdon and I regretted that Coco's virtues of extreme sensitivity, deep with feeling, and her almost exclusive orientation to the relational, was dwarfed by the trainer's own expectations of Coco's intellectual shortcomings.

When I first compared the dogs, Elke and Belam, with Coco, I was more impressed by Coco's abilities, which seemed at first to me to indicate a greater facility than the dogs'. But after a more careful inspection of the dogs I concluded that this was not necessarily the case but possibly a reflection of the limits clearly displayed by their trainer. For example, when she tried to force Elke and Belam to respond on a large typewriter instead of with their usual paw-to-hand contact with her—the dogs simply refused, going into a sharp decline, plainly depressed and listless.

---

*It was not surprising that when the Random Editor first heard of this work and saw some of the experiments, he was enthusiastic about the book and agreed to its publication. However, for a reason or reasons I am ignorant of, a year later when the book was finished he reread it and was aghast declaring: "I believe it's a pack of lies!" He ended the publication process so only a few copies ever got out. I have one of these.

When she finally resumed the original relationship, that is, the type of contact (paw-to-hand signals), that they had grown used to, the dogs revived. These animals then responded intelligently to deep philosophical questions such as: "What is the nature of the Divine?" The dogs' answer was: "Too subtle to define, too subtle a substance to define." Later on, when there was a litter of pups, one simple question was put to them: "Do you want to go to school and learn like your parents?" Only one of the several pups showed any interest in this at all.

The *dominant interest in relationship* is so important and became so obvious as we observed it in all of these human-trained non-humans, that we felt chastened by our lack of insight. We could not help wondering if we humans would ever be able to approach the animals' level of relational awareness. We came to appreciate that that level of relational awareness comes when the bond between species is truly forged on thorough appreciation of each for the other. This is true intimacy and understanding. When this occurs, then communication is elevated to where, in a sense, it is sacred. When this bond is lacking, it is usually because the trainers are ignorant of, or ignoring, the true nature of the animals.

Incredibly, this level of relational awareness has actually been demonstrated by Monty Roberts in a compelling and heart-stopping video entitled, *The Man Who Listens to Horses.* In this video he is shown "breaking" horses by unbelievably becoming their surrogate mothers. Watching this video is a breathtaking experience which can bring tears to your eyes and also make you want to stand up and cheer.

Caleb Gattegno

Caleb Gattegno is the kind of soul who sat down and actually wrote his own obituary before he died. Here is his account:

My death is placed here last among the achievements of this life of mine, though it could be given an earlier spot.

By shifting from death to my death, in the effort of understanding that phenomenon which looms so large in pre-human consciousness, I gave myself both an epistemological edge and the chance to find something important and essential for those concerned with that challenge. Indeed, I brought together the two ends of the duration of a life, its beginning and its end making each illumine the other.

To account for my awareness of myself at any age and at this moment of this life, I had to give the self a sufficiently small energy to lodge it in the initial microscopic fertilized cell which became my soma that accompanied me in this life. I called it a quantum and was able to see it at work, first in utero, to produce the working soma and the accompanying psyche which will keep it going all through life and then, ex-utero, to produce all these facts of awareness needed to furnish my rich and varied life.

Myself aware of itself, discovers what it can do with the energies which are latent in the environment and are taken to one's "bag" to keep one's life thus generated so as to make it one's OWN life. During this process of living a specific and unique human life, the self can become aware of the evolution allowed by one's gifts and the evolution precluded by one's lacks. My death will allow me to do once more what I did at the very beginning of this life, give myself a soma and a psyche as well as a different environment, which will provide new opportunities to give myself a new stretch of human life in which what I could not evolve this time will be possible, and what I did do in this life which helped my evolution, be done more thoroughly.

So my death is the gate to my rebirth and the start of a new life for my quantum to direct and energize, integrating in its attributes all my specific evolutions which translate themselves that way. So, when I return I need not remember anything of this life, in the manner a new species does in the third realm where it lives its new instinct. This integrates the previous one without acknowledgment of the old instinct as an entity in itself. In fact, this understanding of my death has had the effect of making me understand this life and some of my previous lives WITHOUT ANY MEMORY OF THEM. To the point that, like most people, I did not suspect my previous lives until I asked about what it was not possible to have learned in this life but is an integral part of me.

For instance, my will, my sensitivity, my presence in awareness, my patience, my ability at being myself at any age. At the same time, I felt the well of being someone who knows something very important about himself, something only very few are lucky enough to meet without paying the price of dedicating every moment and for years to such a quest. Understanding my death has been understanding my life and what went to make it what it has been. It also tells me that this is the question everyone should ask of oneself and not see death as a frightening abyss whose contemplation can create panic.

To close—what one of my friends who read this manuscript called my obituary—I wish to add that I restricted myself to what today seems to me to be my main achievements in this long and varied life. There is much that others may have chosen instead of what stands out for me. I have been a man of action and worked with thousands of people for many years; I have started working groups which developed into social forces; I let thwarted individuals who were brought to me for remediation, blossom under my very eyes and go on becoming persons with confidence and a purpose for their lives; I thrashed out, in many long seminars and workshops, challenges to our generation(s) and seen them yield something important to our scrutiny; I have found that the changing environments in which I lived could become sources of limitless investigations which would help evolution at this juncture; I have encountered my strengths and given them full rein while recognizing my many weaknesses which needed attendance in my next lives; in particular, I saw clearly that a bright future awaits humanity if we can cooperate in its descent among us, and that summarizes indeed my whole life.

I believe I first met this remarkable man in the early sixties. Sonoma State College had not yet been founded, but the nucleus of a group of visionary young men and women and their families had recently moved to Santa Rosa from their positions on the faculty of San Francisco State College. There were many notable people in this group and as the new college took shape they sponsored a series of remarkable conferences, courses and events—like the exciting visits of Gattegno. Among the many innovations they dreamed up was a radical view of education, which was best exemplified by the work of Gattegno. He was invited to show them what an accelerated learning experience was like. His most obvious talent was his ability to facilitate rapid learning in children who had learning difficulties. He was, without a doubt, the greatest teacher I have ever experienced.

When the University of London, where he was a professor, refused him a small grant, he resigned and thence forth did his own thing teaching languages and math without a fixed home base. Once, in Israel, he was asked to work with a group of pre-teens. During the demonstration of the students' achievements, a teacher in the audience said: "Well, it's clear that these are your exceptional students. What about your students with normal capabilities?" The principal coolly responded: "But, madam, these are our developmentally delayed children."

After one of his demonstrations, I recall standing by the exit and hearing one man, who looked like he had seen

58

the devil himself, turn and say to his companion as he wiped his forehead; "My God! Is this what we are going to have to do with our students!!?"

Once he taught Argentinean Army illiterates to read and write in their own language in 3 days. And I was a member of a group that learned the fundamentals of a very old and difficult language, Aramaic, in a 30 minute session which was filled with his dancing body movements.

Caleb taught Arabic to 34 French people who were working for Air France. In forty hours, they were more competent than others after months of learning that language by conventional means. Dr. Peter Negroni used his method in a Bronx school at every grade level. In the seven years Negroni was there, the children continuously demonstrated that learning speech and then converting that knowledge into reading was an easy and joyous pursuit. In one class for youngsters of 8-10 which I attended, Gattegno taught them factoral ten in their heads in less than an hour. He was no less accomplished in Flamenco guitar, and at one party he had us all dancing those percussive, gut-stirring steps.

I found that the children he was working with, learned languages much faster than I. His highly complex system shunned the learning of the alphabet or individual words. He used colors and sound equivalents for these colors. People were intimidated by the forty volumes describing his teaching method, and so no one read them. It was necessary for him to actually demonstrate his methods in order for people to understand and utilize them.

Caleb said his own daughter read at twenty months and his son at 3 years, not because he taught them, but because he let them learn. I visited with his family years later and found his daughter, now a young woman, was startlingly literate, and the adolescent son was as accomplished and effective a conversationalist as most college graduates I have interviewed.

At one school demonstration he showed us how the electrical properties of the acupuncture points could be investigated by using a simple ohmmeter and an audio oscillator. There was a remarkable decrease in skin resistance at these sites permitting current to flow and to be heard audibly as a musical tone. Another probe, when pushed against the forehead or even one's shin bone could show an oscillation in such a way that we listeners could easily distinguish familiar melodies that the subject was thinking of. He also used to do a very complex demonstration using a long probe which was held with enough tension to bow it over the skin near the elbow. This elicited an audible frequency which could be heard by the subject as a musical sound. This phenomenon was developed further by a physicist who devised a hearing aid which was so small that he claimed that it could be placed in a false tooth. This man had a breadth of interests and talents that were mind boggling.

Over the few years in the early 80s when I was in close touch with Caleb I know that, apparently with very little effort, his mastery of languages jumped from 42 to 50. He did this year after year and could recall vast amounts of information after a very short period of study. In 1944 he went to Ethiopia to translate their textbooks into English. They assured him, that is warned him, not to attempt his Flash Gordon pace of accelerated language mastery on this job, but to take the weekend to get rested up. Of course this was a challenge that Caleb couldn't resist. By the end of the weekend he had become conversant in their impossible language.

He was a stunning conversationalist, very brief and to the point with as much detail as was demanded by the student and the particular discipline. In one quiet moment when he and I were in a room alone, he made an amazing confession. He clearly described a memory which revealed an early sense of self, almost from the moment of birth, and continued on through his whole life as a thread of consciousness. This "master of the mind" was the brightest human being I ever met in all of my travels.

Russell Targ and Jane Katra

I had followed Russell's work with remote viewing for years before he began his fascinating collaboration with Jane Katra. When Russell was diagnosed with metastatic cancer, he asked for Dr. Katra's help. Russell was sickly pale, and he had lost a noticeable amount of weight. After weeks of testing, the doctors treating him told him to put his affairs in order and to begin chemotherapy at once. Instead of following their protocol, he contacted Dr. Katra, whom he had met at Parapsychology Association conferences, and asked her if she would work with him in the dual roles of spiritual healer and immune system coach. Jane worked with Russell exploring the theory of changing the host so that the disease could no longer recognize him. She recommended changes affecting the physical body, as well as changes in attitudes, emotional expression, and social and spiritual connections. In addition, Jane did many healing meditations with Russell, and taught him to focus his thoughts with self-healing imagery and affirmations. She encouraged him to try many new and unfamiliar behaviors: early morning jogging, and expressions of gratitude such as saying a prayer at mealtime. Together they successfully changed the outcome of Russell's illness. Subsequent blood tests and x-rays showed no indication of disease.

Russell Targ was a pioneer in the development of the laser. He is presently a senior staff scientist, pursuing the peaceful applications of lasers for remote sensing of the wind at the Lockheed Martin Research & Development Laboratory. He was also a co-founder of the Stanford Research Institute (SRI International) remote-viewing ESP Program. Targ conducted a series of experiments for the CIA during the Cold War, which have only recently been declassified—"ESPionage".

Psychic abilities and remote viewing are probes into what Carl Jung called our collective unconscious, and what the authors call our community of spirit. The reason we have a passion for our work with psi is that it allows us, as scientists, to keep one foot firmly in the materialistic twenty-first century, and at least one toe in the "Divine." We believe scientists will not come to a full understanding of the nature of consciousness until they recognize that there is no real separation between the observer and the so-called outside world they think they're observing. It's not an exaggeration, in our opinion, to say that the reliable laboratory demonstration by worldwide parapsychological researchers of our human connectedness is an accomplishment on a par with the most notable scientific achievements of the twentieth century.

Dr. Jane Katra has been a practicing spiritual healer for more than twenty years using her gift to heal and alleviate pain in others, both nearby and at a distance. She is also a university instructor with a doctorate degree in health education who has taught nutrition and mind-body health both in private practice as an "immune-system coach" and at the University of Oregon.

In their book *Miracles of Mind* Targ and Katra provide the tools they feel are essential to expand the reader's potential mind-to-mind connections. They offer clues that help in developing awareness of the psychic aspects of the mental processes that are already functioning, but that we may not be paying attention to. Targ reviews his large collection of experimental research and Katra reveals the fascinating story of her own journey to become a healer, as follows:

In that long-ago dream, I was told that the very next day, I would put my hands on a stranger, and she would be healed, but that I would not remember my dream or these instructions until after the healing had occurred, because I was so distraught. Then the voice in the light told me to hold out my hand. So I did. "Stretch out your arm," it communicated, so I did that. Then a most amazing thing happened.

I was zapped with blinding light. I felt a sensation much like one I experienced when I was four, when I stuck some wires into an electrical outlet. A powerful surge of electrifying current passed down my arm, and coursed through my entire body, with a whoosh. An explosion of light erupted within me. Fireworks went off inside my head. I was stunned, and overcome by the brightness. I felt like I had no body. I was radiating light. I was pure energy. I was elation.

I awoke to find myself standing in the middle of the room. I knew it was no longer night by the light coming through the windows. My right arm was outstretched above me. My nightgown was sopping and clung to my wet body as tears rolled down my face. I felt absolutely energized. Completely alert. Blissfully radiant. Ecstatic. Not at all like a person who had been tormented by unrelenting pain for days. Not at all like someone who hadn't been sleeping well, or hadn't eaten anything in recent memory. All the pain I'd felt the previous night was gone.

I decided I must say a last good-bye to Thelma and Alex. I couldn't leave the Philippines before I had thanked them for being so accepting of me. The elevator door opened, and I stepped out into a small sitting area. As I headed towards Thelma's room, I noticed a woman lying on a couch, off to one side of the hallway. As I approached her, I saw that she was agitated. As I came closer, I heard her groan, and I sensed that she was not well. I asked, "Are you all right?" And she said, "No," that she had been having a horrible migraine headache for two days, that she was nauseated and dizzy and couldn't walk, and that she was in agony. Her husband had gone to look for a doctor.

I asked her if she would like me to wait with her, and she said, "Yes." As I stood there, watching her suffer, I asked her, "Would you like me to massage your scalp while we wait? Maybe it would help." And she said, "Sure. Try anything."

As I bent over her, with my hands over her hair, I tried to decide what to do. Just as I was about to put my fingers on her head, I got the idea that it might be better if I massaged the back of her neck. But she was lying on her back, and I couldn't get to her neck without asking her to change her position. So I decided to go back to my original plan and massage her scalp. Just as I was deciding whether to start above her ears, or below them, she heaved a huge sigh of relief, and exclaimed, "Oh! Thank you! Oh, what a relief! Thank you so much."

I was totally taken aback. "But I haven't done anything yet! I was just about to start!" She quickly exclaimed, "Oh, yes, you did! I felt it when you brought your hands near. I felt the surge of energy! It felt so wonderful! It took the pain right away! My head felt so light. It was such a relief! It felt like your hands opened a dam, and all the pain just poured out! Thank you so much!"

Then I remembered my dream from the night before. It all came back to me. And I shook my head in disbelief at what I'd done, and thought to myself, "You were right. I did do it! And she was a perfect stranger!" I looked at my hands and wondered why I hadn't felt any energy leaving them, if the woman had felt energy flowing into her. If I had done something, wouldn't I know it? How could something like that happen, with my body, without my knowledge? Who was doing this? What was going on? I was more bewildered than ever.

In their second book *The Heart of the Mind*, Targ and Katra differentiate between the kind of perception that is normally defined by a sense of separation and an expanded state of awareness which connects with the unity (God). This is the experience of the "heart of the mind." This realization is only possible when the need to control, which shows up as aggression, judgments, insisting on outcomes, being right, and fear or defensiveness has been transformed by a sense of deep trust.

Targ reexamines prayer from a scientific point of view, reminding the reader that we create ourselves by what we pay attention to or we become what we meditate on. If we aim at merging our separate mind with the infinite then we become re-created or re-born in that consciousness which is pure bliss. He has collected from ancient and modern sources all the evidence necessary for the changing of one's mind or focus by ordinary non-religious means and thus has built a long-sought-for bridge between hard science and the Divine.

(As of this printing, both Russell Targ and Jane Katra are actively engaged in their professions.)

Adrian Boshier &
Raymond Dart

An almost world-shaking set of coincidences, perhaps some would call them miracles, were played out between Europe and Africa when Professor Raymond Dart met Adrian Boshier.

The scene began when, in 1923, Dart, only 30 years old and ensconced in London, , was offered a post in Johannesburg, taking over the anatomy department in a new and not well-quipped University of the Witwatersrand. The idea of uprooting himself and his wife Dora, leaving the world's center of medicine, for the questionable benefits of this post thousands of miles away, gave him strong doubts. He did not want to go to Africa. He went. But what was to happen there was surely beyond his wildest dreams.

The next scene begins years later with Boshier, born in 1939. He was evacuated to U.S. during the war and returned to Europe in 1946. Enrolled in an "outward bound" school, he got a start in learning how to take care of himself and being self-sufficient. This fit in very well with his personality. He became enamored with books about Old Africa. He devoured any and all information about undeveloped Africa, the wilderness with its ways, its peoples, its animals and plants. He, like the genius he was, was consumed with his dream: to travel alone there to retrace some of Livingstone's pathways into the deep. Totally unlike Dart, he burned with desire to go to Africa and was unable to.

Then one of the miracles occurred for Boshier. When he was 16, unbelievably his family pulled up stakes in order for his stepfather to take a teaching post in South

Africa. When they arrived, Boshier could barely let the dust settle. His inner genius now exploded into action. In only days, armed with his favorite knife and a bag of salt, he took off, walking and hitchhiking until he was deep in the bush. For most of the next six years he was there, traveling by himself, penetrating ever deeper into the wilds.

Surviving, often by the skin of his teeth, all the time accumulating vast stores of knowledge, he found he did not need to possess what attracted him but only to relate to it at every turn possible. He wished to belong to Africa's wilds by a sort of *mystical connectedness.* He learned much from tribal peoples and was able to gain their acceptance of him. They shared their deep secrets and rituals with him for two special reasons: the first was his fascination with snakes and his ability to handle the most deadly of them, so deadly that one bite would cause almost instant death. His reputation for this preceded him as he pressed on. Second, beyond his control, he gained trust from the tribesmen in a most unhealthy way. They were in awe of him because of his epileptic seizures which marked him in their esteem, calling him a "man of the spirit."

The scene is now set for another amazing coincidence. By 1962 Boshier had spent most of six years in the bush, and Professor Dart, retired in 1958 at age 65, was still at the university, still active and internationally acclaimed. The university, in 1956, had already founded the Institute For the Study of Man in Africa in his honor.

That was a far cry from his earlier years. When he was only in his 30's, his reputation, and more than that, his genius, had burst upon the scene and had shocked, excited and dismayed paleontologists throughout the world because of a chance occurrence.

That took place when he was sent two boxes of fossils which he received just as he was about to appear at a wedding. Unmindful of his finery, he ripped open one of the boxes and tore away the wrappings. He found he had uncovered a one-to-two-million-year-old fossilized skull of a *bipedal, erect hominoid* infant. As he held it in his hands, the genius within him knew immediately that he was holding a treasure. With his acute and almost-intuitive knowledge, he then and there identified the skull as *a human precursor*. It has been called the long-sought missing link.

He was ecstatic and certain that it was one of the most significant fossils ever found. His announcement was for the most part dismissed and even ridiculed. It was not until supportive evidence twelve years later that the smoke cleared and controversy put to rest and Dart was finally vindicated. (A sorry example of not-scientific behavior and thinking from scientists)

Now, still engrossed in his work in an old army hut on campus, he had his collection of bones, tens of thousands of fossilized fragments all carefully labeled and overflowing tables and shelves. Anthropologists know that bones found are only bones until they can be "read," until their stories of the deepest past can be understood. Part of Raymond Dart's genius was that he could read bones. Those who knew him recognized his almost magical sensitivity for, and insight into, the messages from his vast collection of bones. However, he was often frustrated because what he "knew" about bones, he could not prove nor could others read them the way he could.

Now the final unbelievable coincidence: Boshier went to visit Dart. He walked into Dart's building and into the room of bones. Dart's assistant was there. Boshier told him that he could read the bones. Dart was called and came out to Boshier and was staggered when, with only a few words of conversation, Boshier pointed out certain bones labeled as "daggers" and said they were knives. He explained that they were still used as knives and that he himself had one and that he would bring it in the next day. True to his word he returned with the exact replica of the fossil knife, his own still used by the northern Sothos. This was a proven link, a proof of the continuity of culture going back possibly over a million years. Dart was ecstatic and brought to tears.

This was a turning point in Boshier's life. Dart knew he had found a genius who had been doing what no one else in the world was able to do, living in the wilds of Africa and participating in the rituals and ways of the natives, while reporting and collecting priceless prehistoric artifacts. And this was exactly what Boshier needed, a focus for his wanderings and an understanding of his importance for Dart's research.

A compact was made between them. Dart became his teacher and would tell him what to read and how to find meaning in what he read. He also found funds for Boshier, who now had the economic security essential for carrying out his mission. Dart told him he would withdraw his teaching and his help if Boshier did not keep on traveling in the bush and keeping records as he had been doing. The difference was that he would be expected to return periodically with his information for Dart. Boshier found it hard to believe that he would be paid for following his passion, for satisfying his desire to continue forging that mystical connectedness with Africa. Eventually he gathered enough significant material to justify being appointed Field Officer to the Museum of Man and Science in Johannesburg. His work with Dart helped make history in archeology.

This collaboration unfortunately ended prematurely when Boshier died in the bush from severe epileptic seizures at age 39, November 1978. Raymond Dart died in November 1988, aged 95. Boshier's genius and his life in Africa is the basis for Lyall Watson's exciting and compelling book, *Lightningbird One Man's Journey into Africa.*

Chris Bird

Christopher Bird, in one of his last writings, did a foreword to Bentov's (Ben) book, *A Cosmic Book,* completed by his wife Mirtala and published soon after Ben died. These few pages of Bird's are a paean to the unseen reality beyond this ordinary pedestrian one. In effect, Bird came to grips with the ultimate reality of the highest consciousness, or the true nature of God, just as Carl Sagan threw off the constraints of his scientific brethren and delivered his eternal message of hope through the medium of his heroine in his magnum opus *Contact.* Bully for you my dear one and friend! Chris was one of the last of a race of heroes, an investigative journalist of a rare sort, who could write brilliantly and gave his public the gifts of all of this. Later he became a spokesman for Gaston Naessens, also included in this book.

Chris was a good friend since we met in DC during some sort of meeting. We did nothing but talk—we were so full of stuff that almost no one else would listen to. He was a tough, intelligent, big hearted, altogether remarkable human being whose like can hardly be found any longer. He has done yeoman work in many fields and was one of the few of his breed left—an investigative reporter/journalist and author of several major books, two of them favorites of mine. He co-authored *The Secret Life of Plants* with Peter Tompkins and authored *The Divining Hand* which is the best book on dowsing ever written. His book, *The Persecution and Trial of Gaston Naess*ens, is a triumph of investigative journalism. He always followed up his powerful stories in the news with continued updated reports. And all this without a newsletter of his own.

Bird's education was in Biology at Harvard and Political Science at American University, Washington, DC. He served as a US Intelligence officer from 1952-54, in Psychological Warfare. From 1956-58 he was a Time/Life correspondent in Belgrade.

He reminded us constantly, in all his writings and speaking, of the great visionaries among us, especially in the biological sciences. One of his favorite subjects was Royal Rife, microscopist, microscope maker, and master therapist in the apparently subtle realm. How else can we explain the curing of cancer in a few treatments by a tuned radio oscillator specifically designed for each tumor and each patient.

His campaign to bring water to third world countries waged for two decades and was finally underwritten by Steven Sirdahely, Senior Engineer of the World Bank.

After reading his book, *The Divining Hand*, I now realize what a triumph this was because dowsing, which has often provided significantly important and accurate information, has been officially disregarded in international scientific circles. In his book, Bird revealed that the war in the desert (World War II) was literally won because dowsers were able to find water where there was believed to be none. Our government refused to acknowledge this. William Phillips, cultural critic, says that without a coherent world view guiding our culture we have only chaos, with psychic numbing becoming our modus operandi. Dowsing presents a coherent view from the highly developed sensitivity of special human beings among us. Visionaries and dowsers are among the outstanding men and women of vision whose significant contributions I wish to acknowledge, along with their brothers working unconventionally in science, art, and medicine.

Itzhak Bentov

Itzhak Bentov was born in Humenne, Czechoslovakia. During World War II, while his parents and two brothers remained in Czechoslovakia, he was brought to Israel by the British, as Israel was then a British Protectorate. An American woman had paid Hitler for the lives of some Jewish children from occupied East European countries, and they were allowed to be taken to Israel. They were dumped in the middle of the Negev Desert and told to build a kibbutz. So Ben lived in a children's kibbutz all his adolescent years. He was there when he suddenly experienced the overwhelming knowledge and certainty that his family had all perished in Hitler's holocaust, his parents and brothers, and he knew exactly the moment when it happened. This is when he changed his name from Imre Tobias to Itzhak Bentov. He made it up because of its meaning: "Itzhak" in Hebrew means "He will laugh" (future tense of the verb "to laugh") and Ben-Tov means "Son of good." When he came to the United States, people started calling him "Ben" because they had difficulty pronouncing "Itzhak."

Still in Israel, Ben was in the underground Liberation Army (Palmach) and was at the same time in the British Intelligence. He was trained to be parachuted behind the German lines in Czechoslovakia. The British were constantly checking the front lines to make sure the people they sent to their homelands to fight the Germans would not be caught, making sure their accents would not give them away (in Europe there are so many local dialects). For this reason Ben was not sent, as at the last moment the front line had moved. His partner went and was killed, becoming a national hero.

Ben came to the U.S. in the early fifties because an American businessman, who met Ben in Israel, appreciated his talents and invited him to come and work as an engineer in his plastics factory. Eventually, Ben discovered his abilities as an inventor and became a consultant to industry, forming his own research and development company, I.B. Development, or as he jokingly called it, "In-Basement-Development." However, Ben's interests and abilities went much further than this work, and one of the areas he studied was meditation, which he took up. He was soon involved in an increasingly active arousal of the energies of kundalini in himself and began a detailed study of this phenomenon in his well-equipped laboratory.

Ben and I first met on a life-changing trip to Hiroshi Motoyama's lab in Japan. It happened that George Meek's group of scientists were scheduled to visit there, stopping first at the Philippines and then Japan. One member had to drop out so Ben became our Dark Horse. How fortunate for us and how prophetic for Ben and me. We were immediately simpatico. We connected like two lost brothers, and this was so even when he became very successful and famous. At first, on the long air trip, the things he said were very modest and obviously toned down, but as we continued to talk, the utter magnificence of what this astounding, really impossible and most unlikely man was about, started to emerge. I almost instantly recognized his genius and, fascinated by it all, persuaded Ben to come back west as soon as possible with his wife, Mirtala.

In the Philippines, in his first public speaking engagement, he just sat in the middle of the floor, talking and talking from his heart. He was so lovely. He bridged some gap inside of me, and everyone who was present, which connected us with our own awareness of the dimensions of the cosmic.

At one time he described to us his 'flights' (really translocation of consciousness or fully awake OOB), and then he discussed his views of the universe which were nothing less than awesome. And as the model of the state that he was speaking of came forth, like the opening of a flower, the impact of all this suddenly struck me, and apparently some of the others there, and we began to stare at each other in amazement.

It was interesting to watch him with an American who asked him for help in healing her severe headaches. Ben's response was that these headaches were caused by the multiplicity of spirits (entities mostly negative which were always present in this old culture) and that she should leave and go home to the U.S.A.

There were many side trips to see all the better-known healers. One of my high points was at dinner when I sat next to the most prominent healer "Tony" Agpaoa. He described the training of healers so that eventually they could start fires at some distance by mental means alone. But this could happen, he said, only when they learned to let their hands become independent, cut loose of their owners' minds. There were other nationalities among us who regaled us with more or less believable stories. The air teemed with this dimension.

Set against this background, it became apparent to us that Ben really lived from a point of view that was fully integrated with his emerging awareness of the spiritual, or unseen dimension of existence. No big fanfare and talk about it. He knew—and he helped me know what I thought I had forgotten.

Sometime during this journey, I recalled that I had been told two years earlier by Stewart, a trance medium reader south of London, that I would take a trip to Japan and would write a successful book as a result of it. As I have explained, this trip was a crucial turning point in the lives of all of us.

For Ben, the special attraction in Japan was Motoyama and his laboratory. Ben's goal in going there was to repeat and confirm his own lab findings. Motoyama's laboratory was reputed to be the best in the world—excluding those top-secret Government installations in the USSR and the US.

Motoyama had agreed at our first meeting to repeat those experiments in his superbly-equipped laboratory. However, as the days passed, Ben and I started to get anxious because Motoyama showed no sign of proceeding with the experiments. So, on the last possible day to do this, we had a meeting with Motoyama and his American assistant. After a good deal of back and forth, Motoyama finally took off his suit coat and put on his lab jacket. The four of us then proceeded with these epic experiments.

Bentov had the intrinsic physiologic skill, yes genius, to cause his body to go into a highly-resonant state at will. This enabled him to successfully record wave-form signatures of this highly-resonant state which were reflected by actual micro-movements in his soma and head. He demonstrated that the body is capable of a highly-resonant state, in which the pulse and cerebral-spinal fluid become synchronized with the breath, producing micro-movements which induce an electro-magnetic flow he described as a feeling of bliss or ecstasy.

He had posited, in the beginning of his own experimentation, that the fully developed reflections of these resonances would be measurable by the magnetometers that were available at that time, but it would be necessary to measure and study these bits of esoteric physiology on both sides of one's head as they were of equal and opposite polarity. So it was necessary to record these minute pulses with two sensors placed on both sides of the head so that each of the elements would be clearly discerned.

These micro-movements arise from an intuitive capacity to coordinate the breath and the heart-beat so that a resonant wave is encouraged. Ben hypothesized that in this state a discrete magnetic field is created in each hemisphere of the brain, which stimulates the center of ecstasy deep in the brain's core. This results in the amplification of the electro-magnetic current in the brain which he theorized would be measurable by a super sensitive magnetometer.

Ben built a sensitometer for me that was designed to imitate these micro-magnetic-electrical discharges by applying a pulsing magnetic field to either side of the head. Those inclined towards kundalini arousal would report significant subjective effects. He experimented with this device with a modest number of subjects, and I did likewise. One sensitive physician, after a few applications, reported that he had dreamed in full color for the first time ever. Other more bizarre visual effects were also reported. About one out of every ten persons was similarly responsive to this magnetic stimulator and readily reported all these various effects.

Ben's highly-resonant states probably echoed the attainment of the various samadhis professed by great realized beings in the past, souls of great genius and those closest to ultimate liberation. (Similar states are undoubtedly found in certain dissociated persons, or what we Western physicians call the mentally ill among us, but these experiences differ in that they are uncontrolled and largely negative.)

When we finally repeated Ben's experiments in Motoyama's laboratory, most if not all of this original thinker's theories were, in my view, confirmed. But more than confirmation took place. By placing an accelerometer on each side of the head, we uncovered a 25% differential in the amplitude of the micro-movements on the left and right hemispheres of his brain. The strip-tape record was the concrete evidence of our own observations which showed remarkable anomalies and synchronicities. This was a completely unexpected finding yet to be fully understood and begs to be researched in greater depth in the future.

During that week in Japan, Ben and I were able to spend some time alone. Once free of the chaos of the large group of scientists, mostly all talking at once, we were able to speak at length about Ben's knowledge and experience of the kundalini.

Back in the U.S., I made arrangements for a fundraising event which was held at Henry Dakin's. Forty or so people contributed to cover Ben's expenses to come to the West Coast.

It was also during this period that I started thinking about writing a book which would include my own medically and sociologically oriented description of Ben's work. I felt a conservator's responsibility to him. I was well-placed professionally and had many of the same interests and inclinations. It seemed I was the proper person to offer this very specialized perspective on Ben's work—even if publishers didn't seem to be interested at the time.

(As it happened, I published *Kundalini, Psychosis or Transcendence*, later published as *Kundalini Experience*, privately before his *Stalking the Wild Pendulum* came out. My own inexperience in writing delayed me a year or two and I had to rely on a lot of help. But my book has weathered the test of time and is the leading book in the field—thus a classic in its own time.)

At this time Ben was working with many investigators and meditators. He had a long history of contact with Maharishi Mahesh Yogi, the TM master, and was initiated by him into the Transcendental Meditation technique. At his teacher's behest Ben developed a transcendometer to measure meditative states. It was a device which would pinpoint the moment of transcendence and thus of shift in consciousness. He would then correlate it with physiological changes. This was the basis of Ben's "kundalini model" showing the direct connection between breathing and the resonant state (i.e., "heart/aorta system"), indicating an expansion of consciousness in a state of transcendence. Maharishi agreed with Ben and fully supported him in his work on the transcendometer.

I had taken up TM at Ben's urgent recommendation. I was pleased at the one-shot initiation and mantra they gave me, but the process that Maharishi was teaching to produce the goal of levitation was, more often than not, arousing kundalini energies that apparently distracted his followers more than their brief and often bumpy flight. Later I had many patients who became moderately disturbed (especially if they displayed any talent for trancing in meditation) while practicing TM. Some had to stop or change to other methods of meditation. I was disappointed to see that their organization never developed any facility to assist their practitioners when the arousal of the kundalini energies would occur. Ben was also aware of and upset by this situation. It was his initiative that gave rise to what eventually became the "Spiritual emergency network," to help what Ben called "Kundalini Casualties."

Even though Maharishi had great respect and admiration for Ben and his work, it is my opinion that Maharishi was disturbed by Ben's pioneering work with the kundalini and by Ben's doing healing, a gift which was given to him in his very deep meditations. I think it likely that the Guru himself had some initial kundalini experiences which were disturbing to him and which were never resolved. For whatever reasons, he quickly dismissed all kundalini phenomena as a nuisance which potentially threatened his levitation program. I became disenchanted and soon left the TM movement.

This did not interfere with Ben's work and research. Mirtala writes, *Ben loved his independence and never wanted to be a part of Maharishi's 'entourage' of scientists, although he did meet and talk with them.*

The most important aspect of Ben's work is his Model of the Universe. Important as his kundalini model was, it does not compare in significance to his perception of the structure of the Universe, its creation and its meaning. This perception is expressed in the subtitles of his talks and seen in the video, "FROM ATOM TO COSMOS—Consciousness as a New Model of the Universe."

Here is a brief summary of this model: "A bounded structure, like a smoke ring or torus, with white/black holes in the center. The singularity between them transmutes matter, which has been drawn into the black hole as gravitational collapse, and re-emerges from the white hole as a new universe. It's a continuous birth and death of the Universe.

As transmuted matter emerges from the white hole as light, it condenses into matter (galaxies) and is pulled back in upon itself by the gravitation of the core (white/black hole). The core represents the consciousness of this structure and its body is the Universe. It evolves or learns about itself by projecting itself into matter and recirculating it, as it were, through itself. This process causes the expansion of matter at the top of the structure (torus or 'smoke ring') before it gets pulled into the center again. This explains why galaxies are seen as getting farther away from each other. Also notable is his understanding of the black/white holes relationship as the transmutation point (through the singularity between them) in which the Universe is continually reborn. This is a 'modest, but continuous Bang, rather than one Big Bang' and, being holographic in nature, our consciousness is a part of its consciousness and we are one. WE ARE IT, is the final message conveyed by Ben in his second book about his personal experience of merging with the Source ("A Brief Tour of Higher Consciousness"—A Cosmic Book).

"The recent photos by the Hubble telescope have shown a white and black hole next to each other. This is puzzling news to cosmologists. These photos are confirming Ben's vision and cosmologists are beginning to postulate new theories about the structure of the Universe very similar to Ben's model (see the July '03 issue of 'Scientific American' on this subject).

"It would be important to add that cosmologists are beginning to arrive at the same understanding of the structure, although not of the significance of it, which Ben was able to observe directly."

The following page is a letter of which Ben gave me a copy. Ben wrote it way back in 1968 to Fred Hoyle, the great British astrophysicist, telling Dr. Hoyle of his findings in cosmology.

Professor Fred Hoyle
Dept. of Astronomy
St. John's College
Cambridge, England
March 13, 1968

Dear Professor Hoyle,

Introduction

This model tries to show that the two major ideas prevailing in cosmology today—the steady-state and the "big bang" theory—are not really contradicting each other, but are complementary and exist simultaneously. This model does not require the invention of any new physical laws and does not contradict (to my knowledge) any of the existing ones. It does, however, offer some possible avenues for explaining the distribution of quasars, the anisotropy in the "primeval fireball" radiation appearing in the data received by the Dicke instrument in Princeton, N.J., the deviation from the −1.5 slope on the LogN-LogS curve, and possibly, the weak correlation between the red-shift and the radio magnitude of quasars.

Summary

I propose that a continuous "big bang" is going on in a steady state universe, where matter is continuously circulated through an ylem or singularity zone, in which it is broken down to its elements and is ejected from there to start a new cycle of expansion and evolution.

This is an attempt to build a model of the universe on the tendency of matter at very high levels of energy to expand through the ejection of a jet of high-speed matter, rather than through a gradual concentric expansion. The quasar is a typical illustration of this behavior.

I also suggest that the normal spiral galaxy can be formed in two ways:

1. Evolution by condensation from tenuous cosmic dust.

2. Evolution from high density high energy matter, which "runs down" through a series of steps, eventually arriving at the same spiral shape, and continuing from there along its known course of evolution.

To support this model I use:

1. The present knowledge of the distribution of quasars.

2. The steeper than –1.5 slope of the LogN-LogS curve.

3. The weak correlation between radio magnitude and red-shift of quasars.

4. Photographs of quasars showing jets issuing from the main body and jets terminating in a halo of matter.

5. The anisotropy of the "primeval fireball" radiation.

The model predicts that:

1. Very few or no distant quasars will be found in the belt encircling the equator of our galaxy.

2. More fast (distant) quasars will be found in the southern galactic hemisphere than in the northern.

3. The radiation temperature of the "primeval fireball" will be found to be higher on our southern hemisphere than on the northern, i.e. the strongest anisotropy should show in the approximate north-south direction of our planet.

For the sake of informality, I would like now to dispense with the "it is postulated" and "the data seem to indicate" type of writing, and switch to a direct story narrative, which suits my model better.

Let us assume now that we are suspended in the fifth dimension, far outside our universe. We can now encompass all time, matter and space in our universe. After our eyes have become accustomed to the darkness, we see in front of us an elongated, faintly luminous, transparent melon shape having a funnel at each end of its long axis (Fig.1). Looking more closely, we note some movement (we exist outside time). Specs of light are sliding slowly out of the larger funnel on the right side, moving in straight lines down along the planes of time-space, converging as they approach the other end, and disappearing in the smaller funnel, at the bottom of which we note a bright light. We assume now that we have on hand an elongated torus and that the funnels on each side of our melon are connected inside by a long conical passage. The specs of light somehow traverse the distance from one funnel to the other inside this torus, unseen to us. We also realize that the specs moving on the outside of the torus are composed of matter, galaxies maybe, and that we are watching a part of the evolution and death of these galaxies. We don't know yet what is going on inside the torus, so let us slice it up along its long axis (Fig. 2), and see.

In the central portion of the torus we find on the left a strongly luminous region, in the middle of which we think we see a dark spot or streak. Moving to the right we see a diffuse gas or vapor emanating from this region, expanding and maybe even accelerating to the right. From time to time we see highly luminous specs emitted by the strongly luminous region. They seem to stay closer to the center of what we realize now to be an expanding jet of vapor, which seems to be breaking up into separate clouds. These latter appear to condense more and more as they approach the other side. About half way through the conical jet we see quite well defined blobs. We also note that some of the bright specs which happened to float too close to the boundaries of the jet tend to lose their brightness. They seem to stay together due to their higher density, and are less affected by local turbulence in the jet.

We now begin to speculate: what we see are galaxies falling to their death in a continuous gravitational collapse, from which matter emerges through a (Penrose) topological hole into a new universe. The dark spot in this bright ylem may be the stuff that has gone beyond the Schwarzschild radius, and the bright region to the right of it is completely reshuffled matter boiling off as diffuse plasma. The bright specs in the plasma could be quasars; they seem to appear spasmodically.

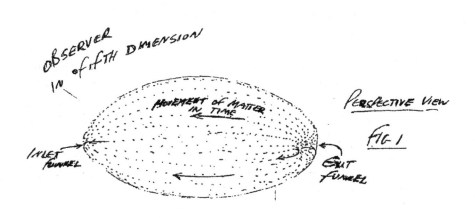

OBSERVER IN of fifth DIMENSION

MOVEMENT of MATTER IN TIME

INLET FUNNEL

EXIT FUNNEL

PERSPECTIVE VIEW

FIG 1

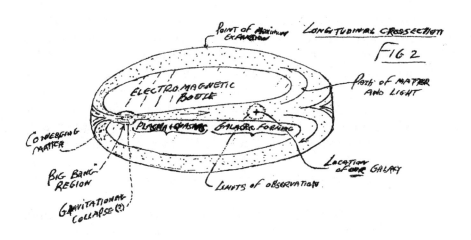

POINT of MAXIMUM EXPANSION

LONGITUDINAL CROSSECTION

FIG 2

ELECTRO-MAGNETIC BOTTLE

PATH of MATTER AND LIGHT

CONVERGING MATTER

BIG BANG REGION

GRAVITATIONAL COLLAPSE (?)

PLASMA + QUASARS

GALAXIES FORMING

LOCATION of OUR GALAXY

LIMITS of OBSERVATION

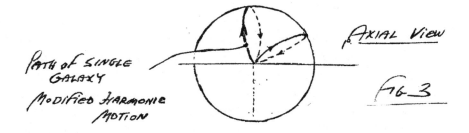

PATH of SINGLE GALAXY

MODIFIED HARMONIC MOTION

AXIAL VIEW

FIG 3

83

We follow the jet further, and by now we intuitively know what is going to happen. The jet of matter is expanding, losing energy, and condensing into more discrete blobs of higher luminosity. Gradually it slows down, fans out into a wide funnel and starts falling back towards the ylem, which is the gravitational center of the system. The fanning out seems to occur due to the lateral velocity component which the particles in the jet possess. Now the matter begins to fall back describing a wide arc, overshooting the ylem region, and entering it from the rear, via the inlet funnel, with a "big bang."

As we watch all this action, some previously not fully understood concepts become clear to me: "so this is what is meant by a 'finite but unbounded universe,' and by 'time is infinite'..." I realize that time is not really moving—time is just there, closed in on itself. The galaxies are moving along the planes of time, each carrying its space with it, and this is why their inhabitants experience time. Although time seems to have a direction to them, it is only because of their movement through it. From our vantage point here, in the fifth dimension, I realize that the trajectories described by the most outlying galaxies are the ones which describe the limits of time and space. Outside them there is no space and time—just a void. They constitute the fuzzy "skin" of the universe.

It occurs to me that time-space, which is quite rarified on the outside skin, becomes more and more compressed as it nears the center of the torus and that this may have some effects on the velocity of light. But here my feeble mental equipment gives out...

To explore further, we will ourselves to the mouth of the elongated torus which keeps spouting galaxies. Here, facing this funnel, (Fig.3) we watch the activity and try to pick out and follow a single galaxy on its trajectory. It soon dawns on us that in this projection we are watching a pulsating universe. A galaxy comes out of the center—the ylem (we can see it by looking down the funnel. It moves *towards the "edge of the universe" and starts falling back (we can still follow it a little beyond the horizon) into the big bang. "A slightly distorted simple harmonic motion" is our conclusion, "if we look at it from the standpoint of an individual galaxy. In this axial projection we see an expanding-collapsing universe. But looking at the whole picture—it is steady state."*

We will ourselves to the inlet funnel facing the ylem, but we find it too bright to look at. There is also too much noise, so that we float again above the now familiar elongated melon. Now that we have gained some understanding of this system, we can try to locate our galaxy within it. Hoping that intuition in the fifth dimension is equivalent to knowledge in the third, we decide that our galaxy must be located inside the jet not far from the exit funnel, and we look hard trying to find it. Even though the whole structure is transparent and lacey, our sight cannot pick out the shape of the jet. Something prevents the light from penetrating through the space between the inside jet and the outside layers. Suddenly we are engulfed in a whirlpool. The universe distorts and spins around us, and we find ourselves back in our familiar surroundings.

I must apologize for the liberties I have taken, and hope that you are still reading this letter. Now I would like to speculate on the above and suggest:

1. That if there was any "beginning" of the universe in the form of a condensed ylem, rather than a concentric expansion, it produced a jet, a stream of matter which was shot out of it, kept expanding into a conical stream, eventually slowed down and started to fall back to the center of gravity of the system, which is the ylem.

2. That the gravitational collapse in the ylem is the death of old matter and the birth of new matter. It is the driving force of the universe.

3. That matter is emitted from the ylem as a jet of hot plasma—with occasional blobs of dense matter, the quasars. Here I visualize the ylem as a pot of boiling and bubbling fluid which gives off mostly vapor, but with the explosion of each individual bubble, droplets of fluid are shot out from the surface and are entrained in the vapor.

4. The divergence of this jet and the subsequent expansion of matter in volume causes us to see all galaxies as receding from us in all directions.

5. The emitted plasma and matter have a high net electrical charge. This, in turn, sets up by induction a strong electromagnetic field around the jet of matter. An electromagnetic bottle is thus created, which will tend to confine this jet of matter, in addition to gravitational attraction. The latter will tend to hold the jet coherent.

6. This electromagnetic bottle fills the space between the outgoing and the returning streams of matter. It forms a torus within the torus of streaming matter.

7. Light will follow the general path of matter. It will not penetrate the electromagnetic bottle (therefore, provided we have telescopes of adequate power, we could see and follow matter around the corner of the exit funnel, but we could not see matter coming back in our direction from the other side of the magnetic bottle). We shall, therefore, see matter only as receding from us. The path of light to the ylem is straight, but it is beyond the range of our telescopes.

8. The interaction between the stream of matter and the walls of the bottle causes some turbulence in the boundary layers of the jet and a loss of energy. The velocity profile of the jet should be that of normal viscous flow, i.e. faster in the center of the jet and slower towards the walls.

9. By the time the stream of matter passes its point of maximum volume (which is at the largest diameter of the torus), it should have lost most of its energy (adiabatic expansion?), and a general degeneration process should have set in. The whole process does not exclude the normal birth and death of stars in the galaxies. It could be considered analogous to the birth and death of individual cells in an organism which in itself is growing older.

10. Our galaxy today is located at about ¾ of the way from the ylem region to the exit funnel. It is close to the center of the jet. The north-south axis of our galaxy is tilted by 20-25 degrees with respect to the long axis of the jet. The south pole of our galaxy faces the ylem.

Let us now see whether we can muster any facts or near facts to support the above hypothesis. Starting, conveniently, from the end, i.e. point 10, we find in a book by Burbridge & Burbridge, Quasi-Stellar Objects, 1967, a chart showing the distribution of quasars in galactic coordinates. It shows that the quasars known today consist of two approximately antipodal groups, centering more or less about an axis inclined at about 20-25 degrees to the north and south poles of our galaxy. There are fewer quasars having a $Z>1.5$ in the north, as compared with the south pole. However, the relatively tight group of $Z>1.5$ quasars in the north is surrounded by a large concentric group of slower quasars. On the south side both the fast and the slow quasars are intermingled.

Let us place our galaxy now about in the center of the expanding stream of matter, and trace a few world lines for these quasars. For the sake of simplicity, let us align the galactic N-S poles with the axis of the jet. Let us assume the cross-sectional radius of the jet to be at the point at which we are now located, of the order of $5-8x10^9$ light years, or just about the limit of our telescopes. If we divide our sphere of vision into two arbitrary zones of slow or close and far and fast quasars, we find the cones of vision for the fast vs. the slow quasars agreeing fairly well with the distribution data in the book by Burbridge

If we take the available distribution data as statistically valid, then it makes sense to expect fewer fast quasars in the northern hemisphere because of their age, loss of energy, and their possible evolution into radio galaxies. This will explain also the ratio between the number of slow and fast quasars. On the other hand, the southern hemisphere, which is the source of the quasars, should have *more fast ones, and the numerical ratio between the fast and the slow quasars should be smaller.*

We may have to add that due to the relative nearness of the fast quasars in the southern hemisphere to the ylem region, their red-shift may be exaggerated, and tip the numerical ratio in their favor. It is unlikely that the quasars will be discovered in the region outside the north and the south cones of vision –a, because of the rarity of the phenomenon and b, because even with improved instrumentation we should be reaching the limits of observable universe in the approximate direction of the galactic equator. As far as the LogN-LogS slope is concerned, it is clear that this kind of anisotropy will result in a steeper slope than –1.5.

As regards the anisotropy in the "primeval fireball" radiation, found by the group at Princeton using the Dicke radiometer, it would tend to reinforce this model. They found a 12-hour periodicity in their readings. Granted, the anisotropy is small, but consistent. It is what one would expect when taking these measurements in the northern hemisphere. At the Princeton latitude, whether they are measuring the equatorial radiation or the polar radiation, both measurements are made in the "shadow" of the ylem radiation. Predictably, they get a 12-hour periodicity as Princeton moves from a relatively "light shadow" to a "deeper shadow" of radiation, nearer to the north pole every 12 hours.

We could use this model to predict that if measurements would be made with the identical setup on the southern hemisphere, the absolute magnitude of the readings should be higher, and by switching between a point on the southern hemisphere normal to the radiation, and an antipodal point, we should get the highest possible anisotropy readings. From these anisotropy figures the divergence of the jet and the distance to the ylem could be calculated.

Speculations on the nature of quasars, their evolution, relationship to other galaxies, variation in their brightness, and CRT analog.

I am starting out on this set of speculations armed with an abysmal ignorance of the relevant facts. This will allow me to roam freely, without inhibition in this area, and whenever unpleasant facts come flying in my face—I'll just duck.

Remember seeing in the previous chapter how quasars were ejected out of the ylem? Let us assume that the quasars are "a chip from the old block", and that matter at such energy levels has a propensity to squirt out jets of material in order to get rid of some excess energy. In short, let us assume that quasars are miniature universes, behaving just like "the old block." From now on sailing is smooth. The pictures of 3C273 show this jet clearly.

In order to draw up some kind of a scheme of evolution, I suggest that the jet in the 3C273 (which carries its magnetic bottle with it) will eventually turn back and close on itself, and will look for a while like the "old block" itself. If we assume that the quasar 3C275.1 is superimposed over radio galaxy NGC4651, then the two jets, one long and one short, with a halo around their tip, would be a good example of this. The short broad jet could lead to the entrance funnel. From there on, the jet will start to lose its energy, slow down, and the whole structure will flatten. The magnetic bottle will collapse (radio galaxies?), and eventually we end up with a tame, normal looking galaxy. In short, I suggest that the normal spiral galaxy could evolve from two contrasting sources: a diffuse gas condensing into a spiral galaxy, and a high density blob ejecting a jet, which eventually leads to a similar structure.

As far as luminosity is concerned, it will depend on the stage of evolution in which the quasar happens to be. When the quasar is young, the central core and the jet are not obscured by the veil of returning matter, and it will have a high optical luminosity. In the later stages, when the returning matter has obscured the core and most of the jet, optical luminosity will be high only in those objects which have their jets aligned with our line of vision. The radio luminosity will be affected less by this veil. The fact that there is only a weak correlation between the red-shift, optical, and radio magnitudes of quasars makes me feel good about this. Large variations in luminosity could occur when this highly collimated beam veers slightly from our line of vision (it would be like looking into the business end of a blow-torch with an unstable flame). This instability could arise from a precession, wobble or random instability in the magnetic bottle, which collimates the beam.

The radio emission patterns could also be attributed to the position of the object and its stage of evolution. In short, we may look at N galaxies, Seyferts, and radio galaxies as stages in the evolution of quasars.

The Cathode-Ray Tube Model

I would like to present an electrical analog, which in some points overlaps, in others does not overlap the model described above.

Let us assume that galaxies have a net electrical charge, a negative one, so that a galaxy will be the "electron" in this model. From here on, the ylem region is the cathode area. The electrons are boiling off the cathode, and are kept in beam form, being accelerated by the focusing coil (our magnetic bottle). The anode region is the other end of the focusing coil. The electrons are notorious for overshooting the anode, especially if the anode is of such a tenuous nature. They turn back, overshoot the anode again, and as they pass beyond the half-way mark along the coil, they start to decelerate, repelled by the cathode region. They lose energy and charge, then converge and fall onto the back of the cathode which has the properties of a diode, allowing the electrodes to go only in one direction.

Ben said that this august figure never answered his communication. This was puzzling to me because I felt it was an important document. For the record, I have included this letter as part of my great debt to Ben.

All this information in its developed form was published seven years later (1975) in *Stalking the Wild Pendulum* and now is being gradually confirmed by new discoveries by cosmologists.

Both Monroe and Bentov described the awesome barriers to be negotiated as one's consciousness goes from the physical and the outer reaches of Earth-space to the infinity of what we can only imagine.

And here is an astounding similarity. About ten years after Bob's confession about his home in Andromeda, I was speaking to Bentov on a similar theme. He said, referring to the world he came from, "Oh, in that place we pass by each other at terrific speeds like we are blue clouds of energy, and as we pass by each other, we exchange packets of information, greetings, and love."

I gulped and almost cried out at the coincidence. In a moment, I asked: "But where do you come from? Where is this place you speak of?" And Bentov, without speaking, immediately pointed above, towards Andromeda. Then he said: "Well you go towards Andromeda and then you go off to the left and that's where it is." Each of these outstanding visionaries had extraordinary experiences which led them to a greater understanding of themselves and the nature of existence. Theirs was an effort to communicate, not to indoctrinate.

But how did he come to his grand vision of the cosmos? He confided in me, during our meetings and exchanges, that he was able to enter at will into an internal, or meditative state and then travel mentally to virtually any place or anywhere he wished in the Universe. It is what enabled him to acquire information that astonished astronomers and astrophysicists. Ben did not travel astrally, as Monroe did. His was soul travel, as he described in his book: "*. . .you ask, 'And what is beyond this?' Immediately* *you have a sensation—your consciousness, that is—of moving like a dot through the void at infinite speed without interference. . . ACTUALLY, YOU ARE NOT MOVING, YOU ARE FILLING THE VOID WITH YOUR CONSCIOUSNESS AND YOUR SENSES. THERE IS NO LIMIT TO HUMAN CONSCIOUSNESS. IT CAN EXPAND AND FILL THE UNIVERSE.'"* (p.43, A COSMIC BOOK). Again, Ben "traveled" through the expansion of his consciousness to infinity, when *"you feel the stars twinkling within your body."*

Being a cautious soul, he was loath to reveal to most of his admirers his superb talents. But I began to see the evidence of this from the utter focus and accuracy of his descriptions. They were filled with the most minute details of the cosmic dimensions of infinite space-time which he included in his book, *Stalking the Wild Pendulum*:

Well, it seems that the real reality—the micro-reality, that which underlies all our solid, good, common-sense reality—is made up, as we have just witnessed, of a vast empty space filled with oscillating fields! Many different kinds of fields, all interacting with each other. The tiniest disturbance in one field carries over into the others. It's an interlocked web of fields, each pulsating at its own rate but in harmony with the others, their pulsations spreading out farther and farther throughout the cosmos.

Whenever a focus of disturbance tends to drive these fields out of their harmonious rhythm, the irregularity will spread and disturb the neighboring fields. As soon as the source of disturbance is removed, orderly rhythm will return to the system. Conversely, when a strong harmonizing rhythm is applied to this matrix of interlocking fields, its harmonic influence may entrain parts of the system that may have been vibrating off key. It will put more orderliness into the system.

We may look at a disease as such out-of-tune behavior of one or another of our organs of the body. When a strong harmonizing rhythm is applied to it, the interference pattern of waves, which is the organ, may start beating in tune again. This may be the principle of psychic healing.

Ben, in his short life, touched many profoundly. Years later I discovered that Motoyama had established a scholarship in Ben's name following his death. Many other gifted people were attracted by his interest in the psychic dimension of existence and his grand vision of the cosmos.

Carl Sagan is full of such inspiring speculations in his novel *Contact*, his paean of such skills. In fact, in this book his protagonist, a young woman scientist experiences what could be understood as a kundalini arousal. I understood her to represent Sagan's true shakti and his own contact with divinity. He stoutly denied this in his public statements, possibly fearing that any such utterances would damage his image with fellow astrophysicists who are less inclined to expand their universes to include a divine dimension.

Manfred Clynes' studies in the physics of music touches these realms as well. I am convinced that one who reads *Contact* with an open heart along with *Miracles of Mind* by Russell Targ and Jane Katra would conclude that Carl came to possess a much fuller realization of our humanity than is common. Len Ochs' work also touches on some of this complex field.

None of the disciplines that I have mentioned here, except those of Bentov, ever attained the stature of a scientific research model. Ben's experiments did this to my satisfaction, but his findings were only barely coherent and convincing enough for any follow-up to have occurred to date. And to date none of them has been repeated. I urge you to read Bentov's *Stalking the Wild Pendulum* and see his model in my book *Kundalini Experience* to compare paradigms.

Ben used to regale me with the most personal parts of his mental travels, these journeys in which he used the most wonderful colloquial language as well as naming all the dramatis personae. His accounts were ornamented with fairy-world characters and biblical figures he called funny names that he made up as easily as he breathed. Mo (Mo was Ben's nickname for Moses whom he befriended and who was his guide, among others) was one of the guardians in this great play of elemental forces that were very much alive in Ben's accounts and that were found at every important transition or barrier. For example, to get out of the earth's sphere one had to match wits, as it were, with particular archetypal figures. And to leave the solar system, still other hosts were encountered which needed to be convinced.

His untimely death in a DC 10 crash out of Chicago was a tragedy that I mourned deeply. But Ben was ready to leave. He was in such a high state of consciousness and filled with cosmic unconditional love. There were very many who fully understood his invaluable contribution to human consciousness, and who greatly valued and cherished him. He became famous so quickly that he often had simple answers for those enlightened ones who cherished ambiguities.

Bentov personified his own relationship to the cosmic realm in quite a different way. His vastly accelerated and very short life was like the formation of a new star. He had a joyously earthy manner and was characteristically full of good humor and kept this extraordinary sense of humor to the very end. He was a rigorous scientist, healer, cosmic traveler, and the epitome of humanness which surrounded all his acts.

Some day, when and if we come into our full heritage of wisdom and love —God willing—all of these beginnings of Monroe, Tesla, Clynes, Royal Rife, Puharich, Ochs, Bentov, Targ et al will become an integral part of our common humanity. In this great marriage of physics and psyche, we as a civilization will not miss the mark again— but will emerge as a society which is thoroughly capable of human love. Only our fearless completion of the great efforts of these pioneers will enable us to truly enter the 'new age' that we have all faintly envisioned.

Comment

Of primary and compelling importance are the stories of geniuses who suffered not only by being unrecognized or ignored, but also by being derided, rejected, persecuted, even put to death. This state of affairs is not just ancient history but to our shame has never ceased, neither has our need for bringing it to people's attention ceased, nor has it ever been more important to our survival.

Aryeh Kaplan

Consider Aryeh Kaplan. Recently my friend Peter sent me a masterpiece of rabbi Kaplan's writing, *Meditation and the Bible*. I had such a marvelous mind-shattering experience as this book revealed in a burst of my understanding how important was the powerful meditation practices of the Jews about 2000 years ago. In the process of creating a great series of outstanding prophets at about that time, most of these techniques depended on the talent of visualizations.

The result was that I began a review of his life and writings. I would like to note some recent developments in my ideas about practice after reading the book. I found myself suddenly turned around in my psyche after my mind blew open. The essence of his discovery, the rediscovery of the key, now gives us the means and tools to initiate a dialogue, a revolution and *a new recreation of ancient meditation practices in Judaism,* all but lost sight of today.

The breadth of Kaplan's knowledge is astonishing. It becomes lawful and a necessity to follow the lead of this genius. If prophets can and have been thus created, it's essential to re-engage this process now, to save the whole redefined keys to the Inner *Kingdom*, as it were. So it may take years of engaging this legendary creation once we have an inkling of its rectitude.

These accomplishments were enough to establish him as a seminal writer, but unbelievably he also shone in the field of science. An example is a footnote in his book, *Torah*, where he notes how the genetic material of goats and sheep would actually be altered by the special meditations or prayers Jacob used from kabalistic sources of long ago. He also worked for our government in physics and achieved a degree of excellence equal to that as a writer and was hailed as the most promising physicist alive.

To my surprise and grief, *The New York Times*, a paper largely owned and directed and dominated by Jews of discernment and integrity, "honored" the death of Kaplan by a scant fifteen-line obituary (on 2/2/1983). This great rabbi, who lived a totally *Torah* life till his untimely death at age 48, had written forty outstanding books in twelve intense years, more than all the best Jewish writers together of that time had produced. I found him on a par with the outstanding rabbis back to Moses' time. For shame, New York Times, for "honoring" this greatest rabbi in our times with fifteen lines of faint praise.

There was also an extensive article which appeared in the San Francisco Chronicle (12/26/2003) on Jewish mysticism. **Yes, you guessed right!** Not a line or name of Aryeh Kaplan was mentioned. His genius was neither recognized nor revered.

Peter Hurkos

Andreija Puharich 'discovered' Peter years ago and brought him to this country to work with him. They became friends and worked together for years. He was a man of seemingly ordinary talents, dreams and character living in Holland. And then, one day at work he fell from a ladder and struck his head. When he recovered from this small concussion he found that he had access to a new part of his psyche, as well as to other people's, places and objects. He was eventually considered to be one of the top psychics in the world.

Peter had such a continuous flow of imagery that it constituted a nuisance for him. When he needed a rest he occasionally used alcohol as a device to dampen the constant input. Peter did all kinds of interesting work for police departments and insurance companies such as dowsing maps for missing planes (at ten thousand bucks a pop). His puzzling death was similar to the mystery that hung over that of Arigo's demise. Now that Peter has died, the last part of his story can be told.

I met Peter at Esalen while his psychic abilities were being tested by Charles Tart. He had traveled there with a young woman who seemed to have very little interest in his testing and spent a lot of time visiting with various staff members there. Her lack of attention to him and her enthusiasm for other relationships generated intense feelings of anger in Peter. Then he became so overwrought that he sank into a black depression.

I was summoned by the staff to serve him as a professional psychiatrist, friend and colleague. So, I went to Peter's sick bed to see him. I found him to be very verbal, going on and on about his sorry state, but not really relational. When he developed a suspension of breathing and signs of cardiac distress I decided to hospitalize him.

I rode in the ambulance to observe him and he became responsive rather quickly. In a few days he was able to return to Esalen. Then I lost contact with him until the late 70's. I went to visit both him and Puharich at his home in Hollywood where he was now living with his former protégé, and now wife, in a stable relationship.

During this visit I learned that Peter had begun to work for President Reagan as his psychic advisor. He had even been given a Rear Admiral's rank in a special division of the Navy with a uniform, salary and all. The ominous and fascinating red phone sat ostentatiously on his desk, ringing almost daily with requests from the White House for psychic bulletins.

When I visited him again a few days later, Peter told me that he had, unfortunately, developed a dissecting aneurysm of the aorta, a dangerous condition which could kill him without warning at any time. He was told that surgery for his condition would improve his chances for survival and so he went ahead with it.

He was recovering nicely a week after surgery, resting in his hospital bed when he heard the sound of an alarm system. All of the hallways were quickly cleared of patients and staff and a big, black limousine pulled up. A man in a dark suit leaped from the door of the car as it screamed to a sudden stop carrying a black box under his arm. He ran up the stairs directly to Hurkos' bed, placing the box in Peter's hands.

Peter was silent in concentration for a few moments. Then he looked up and handed the box back to the agent saying "The one who wears these shoes is an honest man."

We learned subsequently that the box had contained Gorbachev's shoes and that this event immediately preceded the summit meeting here between the two heads of state.

A few days later he was discharged from the hospital and went to visit his Navy physician. Just before Peter left, the doctor gave Peter an injection. As Peter came out of the office door he suddenly slumped over and died on the doorstep. Within hours of this startling death, Hurkos' home was entered and was searched from top to bottom.

All evidence of any contact with President Reagan was removed. Even his Rear Admiral's uniform. And his now widowed wife was threatened with dire consequences if she spoke about it to anyone. She told us that she never received a penny of compensation for his death or his retirement money from the Navy.

And even more ominous was the disappearance shortly thereafter of most of the officers involved in this affair. A large number of them disappeared permanently as far as we could tell. These officers were protecting Reagan; watching Hurkos and watching what Hurkos said. Or maybe they were just transferred to another state.

But Reagan never gave him a pension and never acknowledged his help officially. He didn't even pay Peter's wife the death benefits which he had earned.

George Page

George came to us out of the blue through some connection with the research Adam and I were doing on Project Earth. George was the inventor of an essentially metallurgical or synthetic manufacture of crystals, far in advance of any technology existing then and now in this magical alchemical domain.

In his early days he was plagued by industrial spies and later the government used its agents to try to get his secrets in the usual manner, without paying for them. This is, unfortunately, typical of all major governments. It's easier to legally or otherwise willfully to defraud and steal from their citizenry of genius than to accord them the respect of any ordinary citizen.

He had, through his great genius in this field, managed what no one else ever came close to. George grew crystals. He had one piece of quartz that he had synthesized, so pure and perfect that the Smithsonian would have given their eye teeth for it, and which the Bureau of Standards called the biggest and best in the world.

Others had developed industrial processes in which crystals of a few inches could be manufactured, but none of these were as pure as this one by George. His crystal was an optical flat of ten inches in diameter. He grew them from Silicon Quartz, Beryllium Oxide and other materials. Once, as I held a perfect 10" flat in my hands he said: "You know, in the industry they make three to four inch crystals which are not near the quality of this flat." The crystal was flawless. When I commented on the size of it, George leaned way over and whispered to me: "If I had a 20" crucible I could build a 20" crystal as perfect as this one." This was George.

He had grown these beauties years before and was now sitting on a laboratory right in the heart of Oakland in a 14,000 square foot facility, overloaded with machinery, magnetic coils, and ready to rebuild.

Beryllium Oxide—this jewel among crystal—was made by depositing the material layers while in a molten state. It was about 1" by 3" and rated at 300 carats, about twice the weight of an equivalent mass of silicon. Adam Trombly carried this around to show his chemically-minded friends and it did impress those who knew enough physics. Those who fully appreciated it would either blanch and grow faint or grow red faced in disbelief, perplexity and finally, in awful comprehension, would stagger to the nearest chair they could find.

During one of our more benign presidencies, President Carter's, rapprochement was all the thing and George was asked to set up a demonstration in a government facility. He agreed but on the condition that no one would be permitted to photograph anything. The exhibit was duly set up and George went the next morning to see the goings on. Well, you guessed it. The very scientists who might be able to reconstruct George's technology were there with their photographers doing their thing.

At one phase of these works, George was persuaded to put a facility on Government property. This was carried out and on the second day after the rental started, George visited the plant after hours. There he found Government agents swarming all over the equipment, prying and taking pictures. George protested, and when he did, was threatened by civil suits for this and that and by criminal charges as well. George even became a lawyer to try to protect his inventions but had no luck with that ploy at all.

Our team worked with George for a year. Once I accompanied him in a Pullman car between San Francisco and Denver because George, who was in declining health, could not take the differing air pressure that air flight would have subjected him to. Despite this year of work with him to try and get him started again (he had 2 million dollars of equipment in storage) all our efforts never came to anything. He soon got moved in on by an acquisitive lady friend and died with his secret intact.

Two days after George died, this irreplaceable facility was damaged by fire and condemned. Adam was to be the inheritor of it all and now it was in ashes and no one was allowed into the space. The short-lived marriage of George on his death bed has conferred crystals, property and all the rest to a woman who has apparently shown no interest in the survival of his technological miracle.

This man was a Renaissance person. He showed me detailed architectural drawings of a beautiful work/live complex he was going to build in Oakland, and his writings included a seminal idea for a Consortium for Inventors to protect them and get their products to the market.

He was a jolly, loving genius and never lived to see his visions come alive. His treating physician, who was a colleague of mine, gave him EDTA solution, but due to the inexcusable incompetence of his office staff, it failed to work.

Unfortunately, it was enough of a deterrent that George remained uninterested in any other noninvasive treatment for his cardiovascular problems. He died almost immediately after undergoing an unsuccessful coronary bypass. Adam Trombly's ex-wife was one of the last people to see him alive.

Royal Rife/Nikola Tesla

Royal Raymond Rife (1888-1971) was one in 100 million. He was an accomplished scientist and microbiologist and was the first student of Zeiss who developed a super microscope. Those who followed were Gunther Enderlein and after him Gaston Naessens—both geniuses as well. Both developed their own versions of a super scope from what they learned from Zeiss and none of them had any contact with each other, as far as I know.

His optical microscope could provide magnifications and resolutions that greatly surpassed anything attained in his field to this day. He was able to obtain resolutions that were theoretically beyond the limits of ordinary visible light microscopy. By illuminating the living microbe with two different wavelengths of the same ultraviolet light frequency, these two wavelengths produced interference where they merged which, in effect, produced a third, longer wave which fell into the visible portion of the electromagnetic spectrum.

This is how Rife was able to be the first to observe a live viral form—a feat which today's electron microscopes still cannot accomplish. It is not supposed to be possible to image something smaller than the wavelength of the microscope's light source. That is why electron microscopes (with far shorter wavelength) were developed.

But the disadvantage of electron microscopes is that the microorganisms are destroyed in the process of viewing them. With Rife's system, these life forms could be observed in their natural state. His Universal Microscope achieved magnifications of 61,000X and a resolution of 30,000 diameters. Today's state-of-the-art light source microscopes are limited to approximately 5,000 diameters.

Rife's microscope and its superior capacities became the platform for many of his revolutionary discoveries. He is perhaps the first to empirically prove the theory of pleomorphism, or the occurrence of two or more forms in one life cycle. In addition to the advanced microscope, Rife developed something so astounding as to not be believed—a radio frequency generator which could be adjusted to resonate with a cancer or bacteria such that in a few minutes they were destroyed. In some cases it took a few more sessions.

Even when the quality of humanity is manifest so patently in a genius such as Royal Rife, it was his very rectitude and the highest ethical and moral standards that proved to be his undoing. It was demonstrated when Rife had a confrontation with a doctor, an arrogant dictator of American medicine for a generation. The doctor wanted to use some of Rife's work in order to further his own work. The latter refused to allow this to happen in any way. Rife was told that he had to do what this doctor wanted, or he would be ruined. And that's exactly what happened.

After the threat by this medical dictator, for whom nothing good can be said, Rife was indeed utterly destroyed. His laboratory was raided, his apparatus and radio frequency generator which cured cancers of all types all destroyed, and even his marvel of a microscope dismantled and lost forever. As if this were not enough, he was physically abused by being put into prison, which caused his death.

This terrible story reveals the kind of damage that was inflicted by a single man in high position of power, bent on the evil consummation of personal gain whatever the cost, and all this on a defenseless, gracious genius, a gentle man in all his pursuits and relations with people.

His work was as important as NicolaTesla's and was all lost, just as most of Tesla's was. Tesla was a Yugoslavian visionary whose specialty was electronics and physical vibrations in and around the planets, emanations of all varieties: magnetic, electric, gravity, Shumann resonances, lei lines, hard and soft x-rays. Tesla said:

I anticipate that many, unprepared for these results, (such as power from the sun and winds, and from the earth's fields and heat) which through long familiarity appear to me to be simple and obvious, will consider them still far from practical application. Such reserve and even opposition of some is as useful a quality and as necessary an element in human progress as the quick receptivity and enthusiasm of others. Thus, a mass which resists the force at first, once set in movement, adds to the energy. The advanced ideas will be readily taken up.

Tesla was overwhelmed constantly with visions in 3D of electronic and related diagrams which, when translated into hardware, would do something very real and never before thought of by man. The concepts that Tesla brought forth contained the potential for making fossil fuels obsolete. He discovered terrestrial stationary waves, lighted 200 lamps without wires from a distance of 25 miles and created man-made lightening flashes. He also developed a new theory of gravity, wherein gravitational pull consisted of the net difference between two pushes. He showed how Tachyon energy could be extracted from space (free cosmic energy) and used it to power an automobile in 1931, without the storage of electricity or the combustion of any fuel.

Enderlein was more fortunate and stayed in Germany, noted to tolerate differences in science with more humanity than we have in the USA. He succeeded in developing many substances and remedies of a homeopathic nature which even today are used to treat cancer. But for all of his genius, precious few have been trained in his work. The same can be said for Naessens. But Naessens was a more universal expert in many fields of biology.

I can imagine a heavenly counsel that might have dreamed up many of Tesla's miracles. And Royal Rife's electronic device which cured cancer seems similarly inspired. My educational background in these areas is so limited that I can only intuitively assess their accomplishments, but I feel certain that they both represent examples of true genius, fueled by a profoundly benevolent source of inspiration.

Gaston Naessens

It is a weakness of our so-called democracy that geniuses in the sciences are usually neglected or harassed to ruin or death. Gaston Naessens is one of these as described by Christopher Bird in his recent book *The Persecution and Trial of Gaston Naessens*. Naessens went through terrible persecution and was put on trial for what he was doing in the field of medicine. He barely missed being imprisoned and was allowed his freedom by the outpouring of patients testifying to the curative powers of his treatments which included injections of 714-X and the use of a remarkable microscope. The ruin of Nikola Tesla is another and Royal Rife, in the same field as Naessens, is a third. All of these have been so badly treated by the medical establishment, the legal system and such that most of their contributions were lost—perhaps forever. Their like may never again be seen. Their technologies may never again be rediscovered.

Naessens' research led to his description of the somatid which he found to be as small as $1/10^{th}$ of a micron—too small to be visible with an ordinary optical research microscope. Beauchamp first saw these forms a century ago calling them microzymas. He noticed microzymas had the ability to change, undergoing mutations in response to the relative acid/alkaline value of the terrain. They could exist as beneficial agents or become virulent pathogenic forms which cause chronic and acute illness.

I was fascinated with this research because of some of the unusual properties of the microzymas or somatid. They are able to survive the death of the host, incineration and freezing. In fact, they seem to be indestructible. They are negatively charged and repel each other. They have a life cycle in which they develop into several different forms, starting as a spore, maturing to a sexual form, then a double form and next to their mature single form. They are a plant based life form that lives within our system in a symbiotic relationship.

Naessens took some human cancer cells and injected them with a culture of somatids. This preparation was completely sealed off except for the light entering through the glass bell cover. And these original cells have gone on living when in the dark, multiplying only when put in sunlight. In 20 years they have multiplied substantially, increasing their volume dramatically. He demonstrated that these smallest living particles are apparently not just long lived and culturable but possibly immortal.

Derivatives of this primal energy develop along the lines of their own peculiar genetic coding to finally manifest as each particular plant or animal. Every life form on our planet, and all the marvels of reflex and instinctual behavior are informed by this. Each organ and cell contains these eternal light bearers. They are the first physical manifestation of prana, responsible for our every movement, desire and dream.

In one experiment somatids from a white rabbit and a black rabbit were exchanged making possible for the first time in my knowledge direct transplantation of skin from individuals without any adverse effects or need for manipulations of the immune systems which is thought to be required for major organ transplants. Skin grafts are very sensitive to donor. I proposed an experiment involving another physician and myself. We were to exchange our own tissues to show that what was true for the rabbits held true in the human domain.

If this had been demonstrated successfully, it would have revolutionized the transplant procedures now so risky, expensive and utilizing harmful drugs which must be prescribed for the remainder of the patient's life.

Unfortunately, Naessens was so pressed with legal and professional problems that he had no time to undertake this radical experiment. I am hoping that in the future others will continue to explore this important area. This is just one example of the areas of biology that he was interested in which nobody has ever explored.

He has never had the time, the money or the freedom to fully develop all of these areas. The language barrier has also presented an obstacle. My sister used 714-X for about a year and it's hard to say how effective it was because she was doing so many other things. For five years she has survived what was diagnosed as metastatic cancer and she's still going strong.

It is unfortunate that Naessens never provided an adequate explanation of how somatids may be isolated and worked with. It is a great shame when the fruits of such groundbreaking work are left lying in the field because no one else knows how to harvest it. And it seems to be typical of most of the great visionaries presented here, regardless of their field of endeavor, to demonstrate a reluctance* to pass on their great secrets. This tendency is one that I fervently hope will become obsolete as more and more researchers discover the value and, indeed, the necessity of cooperative scientific exchanges.

Either reluctance, or an inability to pass on their great secrets, is more fully dealt with in the chapter, A Summing Up. It is of great importance to understand the utter fragility of genius. Its process, involving the very essence of creativity, must continue its creativity uninterrupted. If for some reason this process of continuation is substantially reduced or halted, it becomes impossible to be repeated and will be forgotten, never to be reborn, never to be recovered.

Adam Trombly

When I was 73, I was in the first flush of a new friendship with astrophysicist Adam Trombly, and a new direction in research. I was delighted to enter a field that I only knew from an intuitive point of view and was glad to go along with this young, enthusiastic and brilliant man. Any interest in solid science, which he wanted to explore, I was more than happy to go along and help with.

Adam spoke of no grad school, but he had proved himself in his partnership with Joe Kahn developing the Closed Path Homopolar Generator. I met him through my contact with Andreija Puharich, who described Adam as an electronic free energy enthusiast and physicist. Nothing developed from my first phone call to him. He was abrupt. But once such a loner gets a listener, it is hard to dam up all the stuff that's plaguing him. So, I called six months later and we met. And then it was all roses, as De Ropp used to say.

Not long after we had started our discussions, we had the opportunity to meet Josh Reynolds, III. Our talk was meat and drink to me and my half-starved visionary schemes and dreams. And that's always the way it was with Adam. He would propose and I would challenge or question and probe with him to our mutual delight.

We traveled to North Carolina, to Josh's estate and had a rousing week of Old Overholt, technical and soft psychic bla, bla, getting to know Josh and his brilliant brother, Will, resident hermit of their estate, Devotion.

Will lived nearby on a manmade lake of many acres which was held in place by a stupendous dam. This monument to the elder Josh Reynolds had been instigated by this tobacco baron in the late 20's and early 30's. It was erected to give all the artisans and laborers work in this time of economic distress for most of the ordinary folk all over this county. It was a godsend to the economy of the Dobson area.

This remarkable structure, as we stood at its base and gazed up at its grandeur, must have been nearly eight or nine stories tall and was entirely hand made of round stones less than eight inches in diameter. Together with the dam, he had built a hydroelectric station with a large dynamo to generate enough electricity for the whole estate. This structure towered above the forest's ferny floor, as the poet said, and dominated the whole countryside.

As we gazed skyward, all we could see was an awesome wall of large pebbles, a natural manmade wonder that created an ambiance all its own. Josh's home, itself a display of fine craftsmanship, fit the personality of the large man who presided there in rather solemn splendor. He was exceptionally bright and knowledgeable in almost any field one might care to address. And I regret not ever seeing him again.

In the meetings with Josh, Adam and I joined most of his drinking, and we had a royal old time of it for days on end. Josh was a dear character and friend and I unfortunately never heard of his death till long after he had gone on. In the end, Josh extended himself and came up with some funding for Adam's work.

In the research financed by the philanthropy of R.J. Reynolds III, Adam indicated that the underground nuclear blasts in the many underground tests had started to weaken both the earth's core and the mantle's magnetic fields and consequently more and more slippage between these two bodies was occurring.

This was attested to by scientists in Europe but was denied by this country's scientists. There were several of these magnetic jerks in the 50's and 60's that were never publicized here, to my knowledge. Adam predicted that increasingly violent disturbances in weather patterns would occur from then on. Some of this has already become noticeable to meteorologists here.

Of course, even when science knows of these coming disasters, it does not mean that our political and military leaders will take appropriate action. If we delay and deny more and more, as it seems we are doing, then presumably our margin of safety will erode, as Africa burns and as all our collective Neros fiddle on in their boring and alarming litanies of self-indulgence and greed.

Much of our talk was related to UFO material. (For more see the book, *The Day After Roswell*, by Corso.) We met with Jacques Valle, the great French expert on UFOs, who worked and wrote many fine books in a reserved, speculative spirit. One night in Palo Alto near San Mateo, supposedly one of the haunts of our UFO brothers, we proceeded to get quite drunk and sang the night away, but no UFOs appeared.

Our speculations about using crystals as converters from subtle energy to useful electrical current led us to visit Marcel Vogel's lab in San Jose. Vogel's research was partially funded by IBM where he had worked for many years and he had a lab worth thousands of dollars.

After a few visits with Marcel Vogel, Adam decided that such an active atmosphere was no place for him to work on a crystal generator, several generations of which Marcel Vogel had already built and failed to get one erg of energy from. Vogel was provoked.

Adam was also strongly influenced by Buckminster Fuller. In a paper outlining his goals for Project Earth, Trombly quoted Fuller extensively. It is clear that many of Fuller's tenets provided the basis for Project Earth. Perhaps one of Fuller's most telling statements deals with overspecialization, a theme which Adam constantly returns to in his talks. As Fuller put it:

Global vision is a rare gift that must be shared. There are plenty of people out there who are educated to death. Don't allow the vision to suffer the overspecialized death. As the vision dies so does the man. As men of global vision die, so does the race, perhaps the entire planet.

During Reagan's eight years, he visited NASA and delivered one of the best suppressed news bombs of that part of the century. He called NASA "pigs feeding at the public trough", whereupon 50% of the staff resigned on the spot. Seeing the possible repercussions, the Reaganites quickly retreated and permitted most of these withdrawn scientists to become early retirees or to take a paid leave of absence.

Richard Underwood took a leave of absence, during which he toured the country blasting off at the suppression that NASA had been laboring under for years. None of this ever surfaced until Underwood spilled the beans at the Amherst Gaia conference where both Adam and I gave papers a year later. Interestingly, both of our talks focused on the increasingly alarming increase in atmospheric CO_2, and we both showed that Hamaker's work on the threat of glaciation was as important as the widely touted greenhouse effect. In fact, both of them occurring at the same time might be affecting the ecosphere in various ways. Both of us called for immediate further study.

Underwood had a series of crucial photos that showed the peril threatening the continent of Africa. The drying up of Lake Chad, the largest freshwater lake in Africa, due to both changing weather patterns and thousands of miles of forest fires raging throughout, burning out of control, were the causes and results of increased desertification.

Richard Underwood stated that Africa would never receive the necessary rainfall to sustain long-term survival. This was indicated by the powerful photos he had been able to find in the NASA files. These photos were never classified because no one but Underwood, who had been the chief of photography for NASA for 20 years, was able to locate and decipher them.

We worked for a few months with Richard, obtaining a few photos which he gingerly gave to Adam. Adam incorporated these slides into his charismatic presentations in order to impress his audiences with the gravity of the effects of our mistreatment of the ecosystem. Project Earth, a non-profit organization, is dedicated to helping people understand the environmental emergency on our Earth. His internationally acclaimed Website has blossomed into a valuable educational tool thanks to the hard work of several of his talented supporters.

The following article by Mark Schriebner summarizes Adam's unique and substantial contributions to the sciences and to our emerging awareness of our role as Earth's stewards.

Adam Trombly, Director of Project Earth for the Institute for Advanced Studies at Aspen (now also in Maui, Hawaii) has at age forty-eight proven to be one of the most influential and unorthodox scientists of his generation. In 1980 Adam and colleague Joseph Kahn designed and applied for patents for the Closed Path Homopolar Generator, a potentially revolutionary design for super efficient generation of electrical power. In June of 1982, International Letters of Patent were published by the International Patent Cooperation Treaty Organization. (Patent Publication Number WO82/02126).

In 1983 Adam began to dedicate his efforts to Project Earth. The late R Buckminster Fuller is quoted as saying, "Project Earth is a human design experiment. It will be incumbent on human beings throughout the Earth to become a living network, to demonstrate the power of working synergistically with their environment to insure a future worth living in.

In 1984 Adam was awarded the RJ Reynolds III Endowment for his efforts with Project Earth. I spoke to the late Mr. Reynolds during a Tesla Society Conference in Colorado Springs in 1988. He said: "Many people approach me and ask me and my family to support their work.

After I heard Adam speak at two separate International Conferences, I approached him! I had never done that before. Adam has never ceased to amaze me. When you know Adam, you begin to see both the present and the future through his eyes. When you see the world like he does then there is this urgency that takes a hold of you to do whatever you can to make a difference for the better. I could not be happier with his work. We all need to listen to this man." Mark Schreibner.

As the eighties progressed, copies of the Closed Path Homopolar Generator Patent had circulated throughout the world. One scientist, Paramahamsa Tewari, who was then Head of Quality Control for the Tarapore Atomic Power Station in Trombay, India, received permission to carry out experiments with the design.

In 1986, Tewari (with the blessing of the late Prime Minister Rajiv Gandhi) published results of experiments carried out with a crude facsimile of the machine described in the patent. In the American Industrial Journal, Magnets, *Tewari wrote, "The test results have shown an efficiency of the machine above 250%.*

It was the first time in human history that claims of greater than 100% output had been independently verified by a bona fide third party using the description of the art provided by a patent document.

This further propelled Adam and Project Earth into the international spotlight. I ran into Adam next at the largest New Energy Technology conference ever held (even up to this point) in Hanover, Germany in 1987. Paramahamsa Tewari had brought his rather crude facsimile of the Trombly/Kahn generator. The next day, Adam gave one of those lectures with an impact that never seems to leave you.

Adam continued his research into new energy technologies with colleague David Farnsworth. In June, 1989, in New York City, Trombly and Farnsworth physically demonstrated a small solid state electrical transformer that measurably showed an efficiency of 54:1.

Adam then walked down the street to the United Nations to give an address. From the point of view of one who witnessed this event firsthand, I can't believe the entire world didn't change as a result. One of the reasons I asked Adam if I could write this piece is because it is now ten years later and the American people, in particular, have still not gotten the message that there is an entirely new and benign option to the current death spiral of humanity. As the result of ignoring the opportunity that was presented on that day in 1989, the world still suffers under the tyranny of fossil fuels and a global power structure which seems bent on the eradication of all species.

Today Adam continues to pursue the work of Project Earth in spite of the fact that in his view the destabilization of Planet Earth has reached critical, even nearly irreversible proportions.

At this point I am recommending that people pray like they never have before for Divine or at least Benign Intervention. It is unlikely that the boys in Washington and other world capitals are going to implement any world healing policies unless the populations of the world rise up and unequivocally demand change. We don't have much time.

For my part, I want to thank Adam for allowing me to make this little, historical sketch my small contribution to the work of Project Earth. There is so much more I could say but I hope this gives you a better idea of who this man called Adam Trombly is. (Mark Schriebner)

Adam has remained one of my dearest friends and continues to amaze and delight me with his unorthodox style of consideration. I only hope that his discoveries and talents are fully incorporated into the structural changes that the new millennium so desperately needs.

Adam's lifestyle is precarious because he is so bright and outspoken. In the past twenty years he has invented a working cold-fusion-like device three times and was thwarted from bringing it to life by more than one Administrations' unresponsive agencies. Adam is an unfinished story. He is still alive and still unable to get a positive Governmental response to his work. There seems to be an unfriendly attitude toward anyone who would develop a device which would really work less expensively for mankind's immediate benefit. Adam wants to help change, for the better, the face of energy on the planet, a project which should be given a high priority rating.

From my experiences over 15 years with scientists we have worked with, I had no assurance that these men were accorded the kind of security and privacy from the US Patent Office that ordinary citizens were assured of. Certainly, many physician friends of mine were abused with threats of arrest or arbitrary seizure of records by the FDA. Alternative physicians who present too large a profile are among the most vulnerable. They now share this insecurity with genius inventors who have customarily been subjected to undue scrutiny, almost without any fanfare.

Recently I have seen evidence that these arbitrary moves (which the Treasury Department has engaged in for years) were being exposed and corrected. Due to increasingly widespread public awareness through burgeoning networks, many of these abuses were lessening. individuals and groups with money and clout had become active, fearful that many of our eco-systems were fast becoming eroded and contaminated. These brave souls were coming forth to stem the tide of this planetary abuse.

However, in so few years with the recent Bush Administration, we have been faced by unconscionably greedy forces (like the Oil interests), catered to by the Administration in combination with the Military, producing a tyranny which has already limited the powers of the most sacred of our institutions: the Bill of Rights and our Constitution. Our country is rapidly being impoverished economically, socially, environmentally, along with a frightening diminishing of our people's heath, and ultimately the health of our planet.

Here we reminded of Yate's chillingly prophetic words:

> *Things fall apart;*
> *The center cannot hold;*
> *Mere anarchy is loosed upon the world,*
> *The blood-dimmed tide is loosed and everywhere*
> *The ceremony of innocence is drowned;*
> *The best lack all conviction, while the worst*
> *Are full of passionate intensity.*

117

David Adair & Area 51

David Adair was born in 1930 "with a silver spoon in his mouth." He was an early genius, gifted with much, much more than a divine spark; it was more like a conflagration and was fed by another great gift: a father who encouraged and helped his young son's passion for rocketry. A mechanic for NASCAR, his father had access to a huge, state-of-the-art machine shop and technicians. With these golden opportunities, Adair, at the tender age of eleven, built his first of hundreds of rockets which he designed and test flew.

The flame of his genius burned constantly and undiminished. According to Adair's own story of his life and experiences with Area 51, by the time he was seventeen, he was fully engaged with rocketry. With help from his father, he constructed a ten-foot-tall, half-ton missile that set the fastest speed record of any missile at the time. For this he won an award as "The Most Outstanding in the Field of Engineering Sciences," from the U.S. Air Force. After his first rocket he was funded through the help of a Congressman and after his second rocket, the Air Force funded him through the National Science Foundation.

(When he was 19, Adair designed and fabricated a state-of-the-art mechanical system for changing jet turbine engines for the U. S. Navy which set world record turnaround times that still stand today.)

But another event, which occurred when he was still seventeen, opened Pandora's Box. He had built at that time a rocket with an Electromagnetic Fusion Containment Engine. He had used that engine because it was so fast. In an interview with Robert M. Stanley (*Nexus Magazine*, Vol. 9, No. 5, August-September 2002)*, he talks about that rocket. (This event has been written about, transcriptions of it have been made and published on the Internet.)

Talking about that rocket and what happened when he launched it, July 4th, 1947. "There is nothing like it. The liquid fuel and solid propellant engines are like Model-T's compared with a Lamborghini. This thing took off so fast. It went from zero MPH to 8,754 MPH in about 4.6 seconds. It was so fast that you couldn't even see it. . .it would be like trying to watch a bullet leave a rifle barrel." It was launched and landed in what we now know as Area 51, near Roswell, N.M., the U.S.'s totally-secret installation for rocketry.

His unbelievable and extraordinary experiences with the U.S. Military began with that launching. It was there that the rocket ripped off the cover of Pandora's Box and exploded into history and which tore into his life. He was interrogated by Government officials while the U.S. Military was continuing its efforts (going on even to this day) to quash the information, which slowly began to surface, about a UFO crash-landing in that same area. It is hardly surprising that complications ensued, involving much questioning of seventeen-year-old Adair by Congressional and military personnel, indeed so much questioning that General Curtis LeMay made it his business to become Adair's protector and project manager.

From that time on there has been constant questioning of the Government's claim that no UFO had ever reached Earth or had crashed at Area 51. However, from more interviews and through the uncovering of secret U.S. records and artifacts, we can now read about what was salvaged from a proven spacecraft. Books have also been published over a period of years, yielding more and more information through the Freedom of Information Act.

The details of this story can be found in the book, *The Day After Roswell*, by Col. Philip Corso. Here we learn the story of the secret work which went on integrating salvaged alien artifacts into our military and business sector of companies such as IBM and Hughes Aircraft. We are also told about how today's integrated circuit chips, fibre optics, lasers and super-tenacity fibres came from that secret source. The unbelievable facts and disclosures through declassified documents have proved, to the satisfaction of experts, that such a UFO had indeed come to Earth.

Adair's revelations, having to do with "E.T. Technology" and his descriptions of what he saw and felt, read like something out of the most advanced science-fiction stories. His explanation of his work with electromagnetic fusion is equally amazing and challenging. Both this book and the interview with Robert Stanley are "must" readings. Writing cannot do justice or convey to the reader the excitement of participation in the newly-discovered revelations about a UFO landing.

This more-than-remarkable man, this genius, is in his seventies. His qualifications and activities are myriad. Among others, he has worked with spinoff technology applications for industry and commercial use. He has had his own business as the president of Intersect, Inc. He has written and lectured and provided consulting services to companies and organizations that want to know how to use the latest cutting-edge technological advances.

Adair certainly did not calm the Government's discomfort when he wrote a letter based on events following his testifying in 1997. As he said in his interview, he was asking for Government disclosure and a Congressional hearing. At one point the Government arranged what many referred to as a kangaroo court where Adair never got to justify himself or even to say a word! It is likely that after 2002 he was in jeopardy. Word has it that he fled to the Caribbean and has not been heard of since.

It is logical to believe that recent revelations and his outspokenness have caused intense consternation among Government and Military officials. My impression is that he has been "put on the shelf" by the highest authorities in the Government, demeaning him by the device of placing him in the ranks of cranks and UFO buffs or something worse.

As to be expected from the tenor of our history, our Military look upon aliens from space (or even from their home ground, our native Indians) as hostile, as specimens to be dissected and/or eradicated. (Remember the movie *E.T?*). I guess, as long as we have nothing about Roswell except via army people bent on continuous war, that their next move would be to "wipe 'em out." And it doesn't stop with aliens. The same attitude and actions of "wiping 'em out" are disgracefully common when it comes to geniuses who disturb the status quo of the Military and/or Government and/or Big Business.

That status quo is indeed a demanding one. So much information has been held back from the public that it is impossible to gather a comprehensive understanding of just what is what. For example, there is the matter of helium 3 (He^3) which was first found in very small quantities on Earth in 1939. Its magical properties led to research which was carried out under the auspices of our Military. Later fusion research began in 1951 and was classified until 1957. In 1969 Apollo astronauts found He^3 on the Moon in large quantities. It took until 1986 for the scientific studies to be linked up so that together it was possible to think of He^3 as the perfect fuel source. Unbelievably, this discovery has been in over nine hundred scientific articles and journals and has been researched and written about by hundreds of scientists in dozens of countries. A great concern is that it is even now *virtually unknown to the public.*

Can you imagine having scientists and space experts ecstatic at the idea of a fuel source that is potent, nonpolluting, with almost no radioactive byproduct, and is sitting on the Moon as a potential fuel for our whole planet for thousands of years to come? Is this not frightening that it is not on the lips of "the man on the street," not blown up in headlines with wild claims, not the subject of thousands of sci-fi stories? Why is He^3 not as familiar as the word nuclear? Does this not raise frightening ideas about who will control the Moon and therefore who will control the supply of He^3? It is said that "whoever controls the supply of helium 3 will have the power to rule the world." Do we not know in our hearts of hearts, that it will remain in the province of our powerful Big Three? Does this not remind us that, unfortunately as usual, some of our most brilliant geniuses will be acting without conscience in order to feed the insatiable appetite of our power structure. And what of our growing recognition of the reality of "aliens?" Where will they fit into this picture?

I posit that the UFO's have been active for at least a century or longer. Of what significance might this be, not only to us in our country but also to planet Earth? As it stands now, no one really knows whether our planet will remain healthy enough to support life properly, or if it will succumb to the Kali Yuga into which the Bush Administration is leading us. (*In Hinduism, Kali Yuga is the last of the four yugas (ages) that make up one cycle of creation. The Kali-Yuga, in which Hindus believe we are now living, is characterized by wickedness and disaster and leads up to the destruction of this world in preparation for a new creation and a new cycle of yugas.*) There is a significant belief that the UFO folk may be the ones who can help us stop our rush into actions which purposely lead to war and even more importantly which lead to killing our planet Earth. If so, then we would be able to produce a livable future without wars and without the nuclear or other oblivion facing us.

Until very recently, for most people this kind of thinking was unthinkable, scoffed at and rejected out of hand. However, as of the time of this writing, an unbelievable two-hour film has been produced called *Disclosures*. It presents as its title suggests disclosures of amazing information regarding space and aliens. It reports that UFO's have been operating for some time on the other side of the Moon and from there have defeated every action our government has taken to militarize space. These "saucer people" are said to be active in their desire to help our planet and its inhabitants, USA especially. If our own once-acclaimed genius, Adair, had not "disappeared," if he had been free and safe to continue in his work, he could have changed our future and our planet's future.

Comment

It is only natural with so much hardship and oppression that there is a hunger in people for spiritual sustenance. Healers and psychics have brought about their own kinds of miracles, some enthusiastically received and others suffering from persecution.

Channeling

One of the best examples of channeling is the recently published *A Course In Miracles*. It abounds in good sense, clear thinking and is a largely self-directed project which anyone can undertake. It is sort of a running commentary paralleling The Gospels, but it is clearly from a different source. It was written by Helen Schucman, a Medical Psychology Professor at Columbia University's College of Physicians and Surgeons in New York City. Here she had the help of William Thetford, the chief of her department, who assisted and supported her throughout her entire process.

He acted as a transcriber, typing the material from the notes that Dr. Schucman would dictate to him almost daily. Schucman and Thetford were an unlikely team in scribing *A Course In Miracles*. As career-oriented psychologists working closely together, they were attempting to develop and strengthen the Center's Psychology Department. While their professional interests and goals for the department were compatible with each other, their personalities certainly were not.

Helen's overtly critical and judgmental stance was juxtaposed with Bill's quiet and more passively aggressive personality and they clashed constantly. Their conflict resulted in an impassioned plea from Bill. He said that he was fed up with the competition, aggression and anger which, so far, had permeated their professional relationship. He concluded that there must be another way of living and that he was determined to find it. Helen agreed with Bill and enthusiastically volunteered to join him in a collaborative search to find this other, better way.

It was as if she had waited all her life for this particular moment. It seemed to trigger a series of internal experiences for her that lasted for the entire summer. Her experiences included heightened dream imagery, psychic episodes, visions, and an experience of an inner voice. This experience became increasingly religious, with the figure of Jesus appearing more and more frequently to her, both in visual and auditory expressions.

When Helen started to hear voices she feared that she was becoming schizophrenic. This period of preparation culminated when the now familiar voice of Jesus said to Helen: "This is a Course in Miracles, please take notes." She called Bill immediately for his reassurance that she was not going mad. He suggested that she write down everything and he would look at it with her the following morning at the office. She was a charming Jewish-mom type and hardly tolerated the necessity to have this all written down. In spite of her resistance, for seven years she recorded the messages with trepidation, experiencing the process as one of a distinct and clear dictation from an inner voice.

"The Voice made no sound, but seemed to be giving me a kind of rapid, inner dictation which I took down in a shorthand notebook. The writing was never automatic. It could be interrupted at any time and later picked up again. It made obvious use of my educational background, interests and experience, but that was in matters of style rather than content. Certainly the subject matter itself was the last thing I would have expected to write about."

At first she did not know what to do with all this material, and noted that the only contact she had had with The Gospels was through a Catholic nursemaid, who attended her as a child. When she asked why she should be chosen to write *A Course In Miracles,* the Voice replied: *Because, you'll do it!*

"It made me very uncomfortable, but it never seriously occurred to me to stop. It seemed to be a special assignment I had somehow, somewhere agreed to complete. It represented a truly collaborative venture between Bill and myself, and much of its significance, I am sure, lies in that. I could neither account for nor reconcile my obviously inconsistent attitudes. On the one hand I still regarded myself as officially an agnostic, resented the material I was taking down, and was strongly impelled to attack it and prove it wrong. On the other hand I spent considerable time in taking it down and later in dictating it to Bill, so it was apparent that I took it quite seriously. I actually came to refer to it as my life's work. As Bill pointed out, I must believe in it if only because I argued with it so much. While this was true, it did not help me. I was in the impossible position of not believing my own life's work. The situation was clearly ridiculous as well as painful.

Some have wondered why *A Course in Miracles* is cloaked in Christian symbols and terms. Helen felt that this was because the dominant influence in the Western world is Christianity and one of the fundamental principles of The Course is that one must undo error where it is found. Whether or not we identify ourselves with the prevailing Christian paradigm, we have been profoundly affected by the fundamental teachings of Christianity. Yet the Church has not really promoted the values taught by Christ very well in the past 2000 years. It was, therefore, essential that the errors of Christianity be undone first, before addressing the dominant thought system of the world.

There are over 800 references to Scripture in the early chapters of the text. Many of them have been reinterpreted by Jesus himself. He explains how whole thought systems arose out of the mistaken perception of his crucifixion. Jesus calls for us to recognize that we unconsciously perceive him as an enemy, threatening the very foundation of the ego system.

Channeling is usually preceded by an altered state of consciousness, trance state or even a dream consciousness of similar depth to what is attained with hypnosis. But, unlike many hypnosis sessions, the profound state of relaxation is entered into without any self-improvement goals.

I have experienced psychics who work with more profound trance states and, in general the deeper these states are, the more accurate the information and insights are—

more effectively bypassing the ordinary egoic state. One such trance medium in England by the name of Stewart predicted my travels to Japan and the writing of my book. He "incorporated" a teacher (this is a term the espiritistas in Brazil use) who was a Chinese sage.

Arigo was one of the best examples of one who was literally taken over and used by a personality on the subtle realm—and in a very effective way. He claimed that healing miracles that he performed were the result of "incorporating" Dr. Fritz, a discarnate entity.

Jane Sherwood is another remarkable psychic from England who wrote the classic *Post Mortem Journal, Communications from Lawrence of Arabia* through the Mediumship of Jane Sherwood. It is a very engaging depiction of the life of T. E. Lawrence (of Arabia) following his death in a motorcycle accident. In this book there is a very convincing description of a phase of Lawrence's transition that resembles a purgatory sort of existence. Although he was finally escorted to a more benign region by a helpful visitor, the tale leaves one feeling that preparation for these transitional realms while we are alive would be a highly worthwhile pursuit.

Unable to accept the conventional belief system when her husband died shortly after their marriage, Jane Sherwood cultivated automatic writing for two years convinced that she would be able to contact him. The process of her difficult ordeal is described in *The Country Beyond.*

"If we say, 'Death is the end,' what has science to do with ends? Its very existence depends on the faith that nothing ends but that everything changes and continues in a different form. Not a single scientific equation could be framed without assuming that nothing is lost. Let the scientific-materialist ponder the fact of death until he is moved to go in search of what he has lost—the whole range of powers and energies that make up a living personality. Thus I posed the question to myself, but who could answer it?"

Finally her unflagging determination and self-purification brought her into contact with her husband, but not before she had learned to communicate with T.E. Lawrence and another guide who accompanied her on her journey to discover the true nature of the human being, of life after death and of the esoteric order within our solar system.

Human souls have always spent far longer on these planes than on the earth itself; the tenure on each plane here has no set period. Those who develop quickly may pass on within a few years of their coming, and others who mature more slowly may spend centuries here. So these planes of being are really to be thought of as the true home of the human race. The earth, in spite of its importance as a preliminary training for another great cycle of living, is a kind of exile. Here with us is the bulk of living experience both in numbers and time.

Here life itself is on our side. It is no longer fighting a losing battle against its physical manifestation. There is no death; life is bound to win. Of its own nature it is good and beautiful. As it becomes more abundant it aids the sufferer. He absorbs healing from his surroundings and he is relieved of pain as he takes in the rays of love and healthy life from those who tend him. The very life within him cries out against the deathly elements which are harming him and the goodness and potency of life free him gradually from the fever and pain of wrong living.

The Country Beyond Peter's Gate, another book of Jane Sherwood's, is written for the elderly and offers practical advice to those facing the imminent approach of death. In this book she suggests that "alone-ness" should be welcomed as a time for getting to know one's true self. The final stage of life is "a thrilling prelude to a new adventure in living." This book helps in the preparation for the types of experiences that one can face immediately after the death of the body, helping to avoid the bewilderment and sense of disorientation that many people suffer.

Montague Ullman

An astounding example of the psychic energy that can be generated by a group was revealed to a co-worker and myself when we visited the lab of Montague Ullman. On an impulse while visiting Long Island, Freda and I decided to see what he was up to in his dream lab in the Maimonides Hospital in Brooklyn. As we introduced ourselves to the secretary of Dr. Ullman she immediately took us into the research meeting that was just getting started. We learned that this was indeed a special day. Seated were Dr. Ullman and several staff.

There was only one visitor besides us—an engineer and old friend of Dr. Ullman who was the only one left in a group of several boyhood friends who had last met 40 years ago. For a whole summer, these 14-year-olds had met, and under the guidance of one of them, who was more psychically gifted, they had determined to evoke those subtle psychic energies they had heard of by adopting the appropriate disciplines.

By the end of the three months they had tapped into an amazing series of phenomena of a psychic nature that one would have hesitated to claim even from a group of masters in this field working for decades. The following is a description of what they did and their results:

By placing a pen and paper under a table out of their sight they were able to rouse a force that wrote intelligible diatribes-page after page. In fact by the end of a summer of meeting twice a week, they had gathered a stack of such writing several feet tall.

By passing unexposed film in the center of their table they were able to obtain clear photographs of a Freud-like bearded figure with a high white collar, on more than one occasion. At the same time there were unusual movements. Their table rose into the air to hover and bump against the ceiling with such force that it sometimes resisted their efforts to pull it back down to the floor.

When school sessions began in the fall they disbanded and they never met again until Dr. Ullman decide to write them all and suggested that they meet on the 40th anniversary of their psychic club. After this former club member was introduced, they began to display some sheets of manuscript and some photographs. Dr. Ullman's friend, now an engineer, attested to their authenticity and answered all of the other questions that the group presented. He had a very matter of fact demeanor, not given to exaggeration and didn't seem to have any further interest in these boyhood experiments, though he was very explicit in his summary of all the details.

Robert Monroe

Our soul's survival beyond physical death is a subject that has always intensely interested me. I found there are many ways to develop the awareness of our inherently eternal nature. One of the earliest paths I chose to explore was the discipline of 'out of body' research, or OOB.

Robert Monroe was the great modern pioneer of out of body travel with whom I worked for several years. I visited him in Virginia in the 70's right before he began to offer Esalen-like conferences all over the west. These developed into week-long programs and progressed from there to an ongoing program that became more and more refined and sophisticated. The first four of these programs were held at the Westerbeke Ranch in Sonoma. At these very early sessions I was asked to help identify those with a special talent for this work and I was also involved in assessing the psychological and psychic aspects of the participants. If necessary, I was there to help stabilize those who experienced a difficulty during the powerful, and sometimes disorienting sessions.

Evolving from very humble beginnings—portable cassette players with cheap headphones on hotel room floors—the Monroe Institute eventually developed into a state of the art facility. Bob's initial goal was to create a system specifically designed to enhance and promote the out of body experience for other adventurous souls. But his Institute became a magnet for all types of creative genius and kept generating new ideas. Monroe has incorporated many techniques familiar to the genre of hypnosis and has enhanced the scope of this modality with his ingenious use of sound. He developed a method of synchronizing both hemispheres of the brain using a unique combination of sound frequencies embedded at a very low volume, an 'auditory guidance technology'. These sequences of sound patterns evoke "wholebrain" functioning.

The result—Hemispheric Synchronization, or Hemi-Synch—represents one of the most effective systems of altering consciousness that has been developed. These carefully engineered creations have lead many listeners to report expanded mental, physical and emotional capacities. These capabilities can then be directed as you choose.

It was Bob's vision that inspired the Monroe Institute's ambitious and successful program, and in his last book he fully describes their accomplishments. I recently read his magnum opus, or personal requiem eternal, *Ultimate Journey*. He brought the whole discipline of out of body travel to a breathtaking climax in this, his last book, where he describes the whole process in great detail. In that loving environment, under carefully controlled conditions, others were taught to develop skills that most people would never imagine. Robert Monroe successfully initiated hundreds into a process of unhooking conscious awareness from the physical dimension. Once this skill was mastered there were literally hundreds of other exciting possibilities to explore. His students began to experiment with tools that he designed to enhance learning capacity, encourage sleep, enhance the immune system, and many others. His students finally became rather adept in these realms and they began to expand and develop the Monroe Institute in new and exciting directions under his guidance, but without attaining the natural expertise of the originator.

This school had many qualities in common with most of the voluntary adult educational and personal growth establishments that I encountered: they were all focused upon a teacher who more or less acted as guru or guide. But to my knowledge, none of the teachers I knew or heard about through others at this point had attained by their own confession, or had been acknowledged by a traditional lineage to have attained, or were awarded by their own students the stature of full enlightenment.

Years ago when he was a young man, Bob Monroe started to practice out of body travel as a discipline. His initial, startling experience of this altered state of awareness started spontaneously one night while he was sleeping, and at the time he suffered that he had no peers to whom he could relate his bizarre adventure. His fascination with these life-altering experiences lead him to write his first book *Journeys Out of the Body* in which he discusses his struggle to understand the experiences which had altered his perception of 'reality' and which firmly planted the phrase 'out of body experience' in the ground of our emerging modern discourse.

Over the course of many years he became an experienced navigator of these dim waters. After he became confident of his own skills in this hidden dimension he began to wonder how he could be of service to others. When he became proficient enough, he began to visit family members who had recently died to find out how they were doing. It was his wish to help make the process of the release of one's life more graceful, beginning with the stages leading to one's physical death. He would go to sleep with the heartfelt intention to contact his recently deceased loved one in the wee hours. Each time he successfully performed this miracle he was able to exchange thoughts, love and greetings with his loved one in his astral form. Before his own death, even Bob's understudies were able to visit such 'dearly departed' loved ones to assist them, calm their fears and render them whatever help they could offer.

Bob related several of his experiences to me. The one I remember best involved his father who had died several years earlier. In this case Bob came upon his parent in a sort of holding area called a "Recoveratorium". He found him standing alone in this ancient site gazing out of an archway overlooking a beautiful garden. Not wanting to intrude abruptly, Bob waited some distance away until his presence was sensed by his father, whereupon he turned and walked over to his visitor. As they embraced each other his dad said: "But Bob, what are you doing here?" He answered: "Why, I just wanted to see how you were doing."

And Bob explained about his visits to those recently departed. He could see that his father was changed—he was young and healthy and full of curiosity about all of his son's work and OOB experiments, especially with the dying. Soon they parted and Bob left after taking another look at the handsome garden beyond the great arch that he and his father had been standing under together, feeling reassured that all was going well.

Several years after this memorable event Bob got a phone call from his brother. Their mother, a physician, had been hospitalized and was not expected to live much longer. Bob, who resided in Virginia, took the next plane to Chicago. As he entered his mother's hospital room he saw that, although she was quite weak, she still seemed very interested in all the gadgets in her room. This was understandable in light of her background as a physician. As they talked, she suddenly dropped off to sleep. Her rest lasted a bit longer than he expected and he began to get concerned. Then he even called for the nurse. But before the nurse had responded, she suddenly raised her head, smiled and said: "My that was interesting!" She had read Bob's book and had been practicing the OOB exercises that he described. This was just another such trip for her. The next day back in Virginia, he was driving in his car near his home when his Mother suddenly appeared on the seat beside him. She waved her good-bye to him and was gone. Bob said she was one he didn't even try to visit in OOB because he felt that she was far from needing any earthly help of his and that she was long gone in any case.

Angie McDonald related this after her husband Paul's death. They had always been very devoted to each other and one night, without any warning, he suddenly sat up in bed. In seconds he was dead.

Angie was a very matter of fact sort of quiet woman who had never had a psychic experience in her life. So, she was quite startled when, during some mundane task four months after he died, Paul suddenly appeared in her room, standing there in a white suit. When she noticed that he was smiling and that he seemed to be happy, she calmed down.

They said a quick hello and then goodbye and then, just as quickly, he was gone. A few months later as she did her accounts, she suddenly became aware of a tremendous presence somehow connected in her feelings with Paul. But this time she was hardly even able to look in his direction, so overpowering was the vision.

He was resplendent with light and in a white robe and his face was transfigured, majestic and ethereal. She could hardly bear the overwhelming energy that streamed from his presence. They exchanged a glance and he was gone. In her words "He had grown in spiritual stature so magnificently that I know that we go on evolving after death."

Once Robert told me his reason for coming to this world. "Lee, I'm here to find my own and to journey with them to our home out there." And he pointed to the great nebula of Andromeda. "It's up there, and in that place we hurtle by each other like blue clouds, exchanging packets of information." This was the ultimate reality of his inspired life.

I once worked with a Buddhist priest who was finding and releasing tormented souls in East Bay burial places. But what distinguished Monroe's remarkable work is that it wasn't combined with any religious framework or context at all.

His initial mission to me, which was to help me to develop OOB skills was, in retrospect, one of my greatest blessings. As one's death approaches, one's fear of the whole process increases. OOB is an excellent way to accustom oneself to new and once feared territories. Over the course of twenty years I attended a number of these more or less formal training courses. I had never been able to follow up on my interest in autogenic training, an older and very thorough discipline that originated in Germany. I found that I wasn't particularly adept at Monroe's experiments along these same lines, either. After many hours of work in various meditative systems, both quiet in body and very active (as in Subud), I never came close to an OOB experience. So, when I first worked with Robert Monroe, after having done his short course four times, in the last hours of the last day, lying there following the patter of his voice in the exercises, I suddenly became aware that I seemed to be looking out toward my left side—and I knew that I was still lying on my back. Eyes straight up to the ceiling—Wham!!!—I came out of it so fast. I was so overwhelmed by the discovery that I had actually turned in my body sheath to the left, ninety degrees, that that was the end of it! I was awed, and scared and ecstatic all at the same time.

Robert Ogalvie Crombie (ROC)

After I had just arrived in Edinburgh, I walked by the impressive national (Scottish) museum, leaving the ancient and extraordinary street, and climbed the wooden stairs to his upper flat. There was only one large room with a cleverly designed shower in a tiny space off to the edge of things. The shower boasted a single vertical pipe with an ordinary faucet half way up, a circular pipe for the shower curtain and a small wash tub to stand in. He was, it seemed, an inventor—a designer of interior space.

My eyes wandered from the small piano, framed with light wood, to the books lining the walls. And there, in the midst of it all, sat ROC—as he was called—with a full head of white flowing hair and the ready smile of an ageless pixy. Here, before me, was THE psychic of Findhorn that I had heard so much about. Oh yes, there were other outstanding psychics; Dorothy and Eileen Caddy and David Spangler. But I had the good fortune to have been received by the grandfather of them all.

My introduction to this man had come like a bombshell a week ago, when I first arrived on the Findhorn gardens estate. By a bit of errant wandering I had stumbled into a room filled with a rapt audience listening to a presentation. I was soon captured by the intrigue. This was a presentation by ROC about his conversations with the great God Pan.

He was showing slides the beautiful environs where all of this took place and I was spellbound. Most of it was right in the botanic gardens of Edinburgh. I was so impressed that I purchased the whole slide collection on the spot and the tapes to go with it. And now here we were, chatting away of this and that, and he was serving tea. Our conversation was so animated, that my companion in this adventure, feeling a bit left out, struck out on her own for a while.

I found out that ROC had served in the first World War as a wireless operator. Since I am a ham operator, this fact alone made us buddies.

After talking for a while, a friend of ROC's dropped in who was an opera star. The two of them, a man and a woman, sat at the piano and delivered to me a most engaging concert of all the operatic airs I so loved.

In between these musical romps, ROC told us of his many meetings with Pan, God of the nature spirits, plant, and animal as well. It was a thoroughly splendid account and so animated that I could see it all unfold there in his flat, right before my eyes and ears. I could sense the chthonic force of the God himself as he exposed the realm where he ruled supreme. He penetrated me with his concern for the wanton ignoring of his person and power in this realm where all of us dwell. He stated more than once; "If you people only cared for this wondrous natural realm and sought our help we could quickly heal all the destruction your carelessness has caused."

Olga Worral

We had gone to Findhorn for a week and had met Peter Caddy and his wife Eileen. She had been, along with Spangler and Robert Ogalvie Crombie, one of the principle channels in the whole tale of this remarkable group. When we visited there, David Spangler was just about to leave on some of his travels so we weren't able to spend much time with him. We did not meet Dorothy, another star in this cast, until years later when we went to her home in Belmont, California, where she had been living for the years since the group had gone its separate ways. She was a talented, charming lady and confirmed most of the impressions that we had formed in Findhorn and later on. The group had, at first, been channeling material relevant to the threat of nuclear war after 1950. This concern had gradually resolved itself to some extent, and it was during this time of rapprochement that they rather abruptly changed their focus.

The new direction of their combined channeling was, of course, Findhorn. They sought out a place in Scotland and planted gardens which thrived beyond belief in the midst of an incredibly challenging climate. They credited their gardening success to the devas, or plant spirits, who instructed them and assisted their efforts. It was the amazing success of their joint effort that eventually brought Findhorn fame.

Soon we found ourselves boarding the train for England and, by chance, met a great psychic gentleman and healer on the train. His name was something like Andrew Bierce. We had run into him a few days earlier in England. This was our second meeting.

He came to where we were sitting, seized my arm and fixed my eye with an intensely powerful stare, full of entreaty, and said: "I have a message from Olga for Ambrose." (We had worked with Olga Worral years before.)

Now, Olga had died a year or so earlier and this was a message from the beyond received by this agile old man and renowned psychic, for Ambrose Worral, Olga's husband of many years and helper in her healing mission in Baltimore.

The message was simply to reassure Ambrose that Olga was doing well and that she sent her love to him from beyond the grave—the great divide. I was able to give this message to Ambrose and he received it rather nonchalantly, as if he had been sure of it all along.

Beverly Rubrick had been working with Olga Worral and Elizabeth Raucher in an experiment that they had designed. Olga was attempting to impress a virulent culture of bacteria to become less robust and dangerous. I spent many evenings at their lab in San Francisco State College discussing protocol and procedures in such research.

Both Olga and Elizabeth were quite young and worked hard, eager to learn and also to become more widely known in their field. Olga, as it turned out, was able to attenuate these cultures. She was a well known healer and had helped many reputable medical doctors develop their interest in the psychic realm and in the mysteries of accelerated healing. By this time she had already shown that she could modify the vapor trails in a cloud chamber by mental means alone.

Olga had once paid a visit to San Francisco and had called me on the phone saying: "Let's get together and have a seance." I had told her that we had a young Native American woman who was a talented psychic and would oblige us.

The next thing we knew, Olga had arrived in a taxi into which Freda and the young psychic and I clambered. We were busily engaged in hellos and hugs and soon it was obvious to all that the young girl was so awe stricken that she was speechless. In the presence of the great Olga, she could only admire and dream. So, Olga, never being at a loss in any situation, just gracefully and naturally took over. In her most polished manner, she began to give an in-depth psychic reading for the young woman. Her reading was not only very detailed, but very interesting and relevant to the young aspirant. Even though the details now escape me, the memory of the oohs and aahs of Olga's subject never will. Thus, we had our psychic evening, replete with the drama that Olga's charm provided.

Stanley Keleman

I met Stanley years ago when I went to the West Coast and felt immediately attracted to his intensity and passion. He became my first and best friend there. My impressions of him are drawn from our professional and personal friendship which we still enjoy. There was a profundity of his thinking and feeling which reminded me of Arthur Young, author of *The Reflexive Universe* and inventor of the Bell helicopter. Both of them were complex and original thinkers who were only partially appreciated by their admirers. Stan had tendencies, which in another cultural setting might have led him into the priesthood. Instead, he focused on somatic awareness.

One day, out of the blue, he was phoned by Eileen Garrett because she had heard so much about his talents. She was so impressed that he received a grant from her as he was getting started in his specialty of Bio-energetics.

Stan told me once of his first and only experience of instant and miraculous healing. I am including this story as an example of life's most unfathomable mysteries. While staying at a ski resort, Stan was relaxing by an indoor heated pool. One of the guests there seemed to be rather drunk. She was cavorting around on the slippery pool-side tiles when she slipped and crashed to the hard floor, fracturing one leg very badly. Stan was drawn to go over to her while she was awaiting the arrival of an ambulance.

As she sat there shivering by the pool's edge, probably in shock, he came up beside her. Without any thoughts other than her suffering, he was impulsed to put his hands out over the stricken limb. He felt as if his hands had a mind of their own. He was astonished to see that suddenly all of the tissues of her leg became transparent to him. He could see the bones and, as he focused on them, they appeared to be flowing together and the injuries mended themselves.

After a few minutes her pain subsided. Then the skin closed and the bleeding stopped and as he drew away from her, he felt that the whole injury was healed. However, the woman was still quite drunk and refused to be restrained by her friends. She insisted on getting up and commenced to fling herself around again and in a few seconds she stumbled and fell again, re-fracturing the same leg. And at about that time, the ambulance arrived and took her off.

The gift of such instant healing is very rare. To assume that because it happened once and that the siddhi to heal is now available, is one of the illusions the ego likes to identify with. To his credit, Stan has never identified with nor sought out that kind of healing experience again—not that it isn't a legitimate area of inquiry. And he has not had a similar experience, nor has he any inclination to exploit this potential healing gift in any manner, except to do what he does every day in his energetic body-work. I would say his primary thrust is more of a rabbinical one, thinly disguised by his training with Karlfried von Druckheim, the German philosopher and therapist.

Medard Boss was the founder of what he called Daseinsanalysis. Stan remembered him as a powerfully built, square, robust and imposing man. When he saw Medard again, now in his eighties, he saw a slow-moving, frail, pear-shaped white-haired old man.

We discussed therapy and I realized he was still active with clients. I asked him what it was like doing therapy with people as an older man. He replied: "Stanley, what is important in our work is the love of the therapist. That is what cures, the love of the therapist. As you age, it is easier to love the patient."

His statement confirmed my own intuition that as a therapist matures, it is easier to express feelings. You can more fully receive what the patient has to give. Aging brings about the possibility of having access to a deeper dimension of feeling for the therapist and client alike.

Stan observed that each 'age' has its own distinct somatic shape. In each phase of life, there is a particular manner that we shape ourselves to which expresses our relationship to experience. Each of these somatic stages and shapes is a continual process of renewal. He observed that we are born to be full-grown, mature and aging adults growing these shapes from our genetic inheritance. And our shape reflects the ways that we participate in life.

People who are growing into their mature age and shape have specific concerns. They desire to be a part of a circle of contact; they do not want to be isolated or infantilized or treated as if they no longer have an independent existence. With advanced age, there is a fear of being infirm and a threatened loss of a known form. There is an uncertainty, about how to continue to create form for whatever is growing, as the physical self diminishes.

When both the client and the therapist speak from the profound somatic shifts of aging, the brain and heart of both are kept vital. Somatic inwardness is a way to maintain fidelity to a slower bodying process and is a way of forming a deeper contact with our existence. Forming a mature somatic presence means forming a sensation-based relationship with our bodies, not our images, actions or social roles. As we tell the truth of our existence we become more real and we grow outwardly and inwardly, not in passive acceptance of our aging, but in an active receiving of ourselves.

To embody what we have experienced is an important goal at any age. The mature person gathers years and incorporates experiences differently from the young. Aging is not an illness or a tragedy but a quality of how we are present. As we shift shape, we shift the way we are present with others. We grow intellectually and emotionally. We stay committed to an inward self that we share with others.

If psychology is not based in formative or evolutionary principles, then wisdom and growth become solely psychological or emotional events. Formative psychology states that life makes body form and shapes what it grows. Life grows bodies and is continually forming and evolving an individuated somatic reality. In formative psychology we want to understand how we body experience and personal expression. If we assume that we cannot influence somatic experience and destiny, we become victims to the image of aging. Therefore, the key is to continue to form our embodiment. This volitional participation in growing an inwardness makes the mature and aging somatic self present. To form at any age is to be in relationship to self and others and to include past and future experiences of bodying in the present.

Our task as humans, as therapists, is to make aging and dying human, to give bodied life and its subjectivity the highest status. If the inwardness of our own somatic intimacy is present, we transcend our own death by living it with others.

This is his how he understood the death of his teacher: *I sat beside him as he was dying and although he was shrunken, he was willing to share his dying experience. In turn he wanted his presence, his fears to be received. He initiated me into an encounter I will certainly have. I learned to be with him as he was being with himself. Out of this experience we created a world that defied time. It had a quality of eternity. I wonder if this is what is meant by timelessness. No amount of imagination or insight can substitute the sharing and receiving of one's somatic experience.*

Keleman contributed a unique languaging of human experience which was strictly his own, rooted in Bio-energetics and the Swiss-German tradition called Daseinsanalysis. I add here Stan's own description of what I would call the Taoist model of kundalini which is more compatible than the Hindu with my own scientific orientation. His images add yet another dimension to the sciences of Bentov's model, and are a fitting addition to the literature of the kundalini state as I put it forth in my book, *Kundalini: Psychosis or Transcendence.*

Here are Stan's words to me which he titled "The Snake", written in the mid-seventies: *On a night in 1959, while lying in bed awake, I experienced an out-of-the-ordinary event that, for me, brought biology and psychology together. It also opened the door to my understanding the evolutionary process that goes on in one's self. While I was working on reducing muscular tension around my chest and throat, I had a vision of a snake, green and vivid, that seemed to coil out of my intestines and up into my head. The next night the same event occurred, except that this time when the snake flowed into my head it appeared to enter a silver ring.*

While I could say the snake was flowing in me, I also experienced that I was the snake, and that we were encased together in a large egg-shaped envelope, a field of flowing. And then I realized that I was the envelope. I was inside the envelope and I was also the envelope. The envelope, in turn, was part of a huge field extending endlessly in every direction.

Over the next several years, I improved my ability to be in contact with the flow of the snake. I began to see the relationship between this flow and the process of growth. I gained the insight that I am a flow spiraling up and down, out and in, a flow with its own inner logic and balance. And because I experienced that my egg-shaped envelope was part of a still larger field, I began to feel that I shared a universal identity along with my individual identity.

My recurring vision of the snake was simultaneously a surface perception and a depth perception of the flow which I felt throughout my entire self. One day in the fall of 1964, as I was feeling the brightness of the flow, the snake moved out from my bowels up to the area of the sternum, both inside and outside. I was awake, alert. I could see the flow, feel it, yet I was it. I was part of it: It was part of me.

A few nights later, a restless night, I experienced first a force, a pain in the chest, and then the flow piercing through my diaphragm. My image was that of a snake bursting through the center of an orange slice. The whole of the next day I was completely enveloped in a circulating warmth that came from me and protected me. The whole world was warm and intense.

Later on in this period I had two other serpent visions which expressed the same pattern of perception and participation. In one event I was startled to perceive a snake lying coiled in what appeared to be a field around my pelvis. On the next occasion, I experienced an uncoiled serpent rising and trying to enter my head. My reaction was panic until I understood that this was a friend of mine.

In each situation I recognized that the snake was part of me and at the same time part of a greater force—in other words, both me and not me. I saw that I could accept it or fight it off. I could extend my boundaries or hold onto them. The extending of boundaries leads to an experience of being connected with an expanded world, a reality that transcends our usual range of perception. The self-extending gives the feeling that the dualities of our perception are unified in a larger field.

I speak of visions rather than dreams or projections because in each case my experience took place within the expanded boundaries of a large unifying field. If these events were only projections of the brain, then somehow they got projected all around me and through me, not just in front of me.

The snake is my personal vision of the formative principle. Another event will make the connection more clear.

On this particular occasion I saw not one but two snakes. With their tails still in my pelvic basin, one snake coiled up the right side of my body and the other up the left side. It was as if they were carrying on a dialogue, and they carried it on into my brain. There they paused, as if shaking hands. Then their heads met.

If you turn the pattern of the snake's dialogue onto its side, you have the loop of the formative process. The snakes open up from the pelvis and form the body of containment. They cross over once. Then they close the body of containment. Instead of going on to make a sequence of figure eights, they circulate back through themselves and through each other. The circuit is achieved by the snake's heads passing before they fuse. It is in that pause, in that dialogue of gestures which I call shaking hands, that an agreement is mediated.

That sets up the circulation until another area of discontinuousness arises. Then once again there are two snakes. They have another dialogue; they pause and come together again. And so you have a continuing process of describing the figure eight, of making and remaking the formative loop.

Though there are also individual elements, there is a relationship between the flow of the snake and the flow of breathing. Both bring about the feeling of an ongoing expanding and contracting. The flow of the snake gets bigger and brighter with the out-breath, smaller and less bright with the in-breath.

If you hold your breath, you can more easily feel the pulsations and streamings that go on inside and sometimes outside your body. The movement flows from foot to head, head to foot, with storage poles in the head and in the pelvic basin. Movement toward the pelvic basin is symbolic of the return to the excitatory world, the world of excitational pattern. The pelvis receives the flow, transforms it, and gives rise to new movement in the direction of the head which receives it and transforms it in turn.

When I say "transform", I mean that there is a qualitative and quantitative change that takes place in the flow from pelvis to head and head to pelvis. As I experienced the snake rising up through my torso, I would feel a quality of love and thrust that softened as it entered my head. There it would make a picture or a new insight, a refined perception as distinct from a global perception. It would coil up from my pelvis as an undefined impulse wanting contact, then all of a sudden it would come in contact and that contact would lead to other possibilities.

Another kind of transformation occurs as the flow circulates from the head to the pelvic basin. The pelvic basin receives and holds the energy, then gives it sexual and genital specificity. The pelvis contains the flow and then gives it a thrusting quality.

What I'm saying here is that what you begin to experience bodily, alters itself; and it usually alters itself in one of two ways. What you think you're experiencing gets circulated, taking on another quality. That's what I mean by transformation. What you think something is may be that thing, but it also opens the door to something else.

Things are revealed on many levels. They don't ever really repeat themselves. We think it's one thing, and then when we experience that, it turns out to be something slightly different. We're not living in a circle.

One can also talk about transformation of energy in terms of the depth and the surface of the organism. The snake flows into my pelvis, and I experience an increasing oneness with nature. Then, as it emerges from deep inside, moving from a prepersonal place toward my surface, my boundaries, I feel that it goes through all the evolutionary layers, and I have various images. I feel that it goes through space, that it goes through an ocean world and then through kind of a jungle world. I actually conceptualize plant life in a jungle. And then when the snake is at the surface it creates the social world. It's as if the snake, flowing through the many levels of itself, repeats the whole evolutionary history as I come to the new social relationship that's possible for me at that time.

The flow of energy moves through different levels of cellular organization. I really think that Jung's archetypes come from cellular levels in the depths of the organism. Cellular levels in the depths of the organism are related to racial history. Those closer to the surface are more related to our present social history.

The snake expressed the circulation and continuing intensity of a pulsing, undulating flow. I cannot say how this flow is directly related to physiological processes, but it is clear that it generates physiological effects such as warmth, change in heart rate, and symptoms of excitement. It is also clear that this same flow affects the psychic system by stimulating images, forgotten memories, feelings of ancientness and timelessness, and the fresh feelings of love, contact, and anxiety that accompany the broadening of boundaries.

The organismic fullness of the flow convinced me of the oneness of the physical and psychical selves. These selves live and grow in the field of the snake, reflecting it in different forms—expressions of the snake essence. The snake is both inside and outside. There are interfaces between one's inner world, one's outer world, and the world of the snake.

I learned from my experiences of the snake that a basic human process was presenting itself. I related to the movement of this flow and to the enveloping field. In the meantime, it began to be part of my daily existence that I was never without the feeling of being surrounded to some extent by this field. It was bright in quality and oval in shape. I was happy I identified with it. I was connected with it and it with the universe. My personal conflicts were actually taking place in this background, this unity, which embraced and held the opposites in me.

I am this background. This means I wish to maintain my tie with the eventful earth world of here and now. I cannot yet say what the enveloping field is. I know I am related to a larger reality; I am aware of its communication. Its manifestations are different from my biological and social needs. I am aware of it and part of it. I am it, yet my identity is still with my time-space body and time-space events.

In the snake world, the ordinary limits of time-space appear to expand. Space seems to be infinitely extended, and time is no longer confined to a linear progression. There does not seem to be a passage of time. Nor is there a quality of past, present or future. The flow presents itself like flashes of a strobe light, or view patterns in a kaleidoscope.

There is perception and remembrance of events, but the events do not belong to the clock sequence.

The experience of the snake points to a different sort of life awareness—an awareness of man not as the sole determiner of reality but as part of a bigger life process. One part of me is conditioned by the world of time-space and is probably meant to be conditioned by that world. Another part of me is unaffected by time-space conditioning and relates to another energetic dimension.

The process of the snake is a continuum with all aspects of existence. This process operates by its own laws and attempts to heal, makes us whole. It energizes the evolution of our species toward other ways of being.

At the very least, the snake image represents the bridge of the conscious, the known, and the unconscious, the unknown. Certainly the unconscious is not just a reservoir of repressed, unlived past, but contains the dynamics of all evolutionary possibilities. In this light the serpent may be seen as a pattern of growth whose energy gives form and expression to the ongoing life of an individual. It manifests form, or is form-producing. In the ocean of life, and within the species which is tied together as a whole in its energetic development, one role of the snake is to develop individuality.

But even more than the individualistic role, I stress the universal implication of the serpentine flow. I call it universal because not only do I perceive it in myself and in my environment, but it's an archetypal image that almost all cultures have used to depict life's growing and transforming process.

The quality of cosmic expression, in terms of both its uniqueness and its consistency, is presented by the waves of the sea, the double-helix of DNA, the twisting paths of blood vessels. The snake is the shape of man and its flow is the rhythm of his thinking and feeling and functioning—his continuously discontinuous rhythm of waking and sleeping, standing up and lying down, feeling separate and feeling at

151

one. We are not isolated, nor are we floundering: the universe has direction.

When I talked to him recently he said that this experience had radically changed his life in ways which were subtle and which are still revealing themselves to him.

Miraculous Healing in Brazil

I was in a group of scientists, mostly MD's and engineers, who visited the Far East. The first leg of our trip was the Philippines. We had many side trips to see all the better-known healers but saw no truly remarkable healings during our stay. At one dinner I sat next to the most prominent healer, "Tony Agpoa," who described the training of the healers so that eventually they could start fires at some distance by mental means alone. But they needed first to learn to let their hands become independent or cut loose of their owners' minds, a discipline requiring a high degree of proficiency. This small experience made very little difference in my life. However, my journey to Brazil was intensely spiritual and healing and I felt associated with the great healer who came from a long line of Jewish prophets. Here I will recount my experience:

Some 2,000 years ago, a mythical figure arose from the Jewish prophets, of whom there were many, one singularity, having all the virtues of sainthood. Beloved of God, blessed with the gift of healing that men and women might delight the eyes and hearts of all.

Even the dead sea scrolls confirm parts of this remarkable arising, which is all but lost among similar aboriginal figures before the findings of archeology emerged—also before those Phoenician clay tablets and the magic of Gilgamesh and Inkidoo ignited the hearts and minds of men.

Since then, many native healers of lesser stature than Jesus continued to become known. Then suddenly, fully recorded by scientists, two souls in the tradition of the Esperitistas of Brazil and the Philippines became known and celebrated.

First, Arigo in the sixties, and then Joao of God in the nineties. Arigo began his short life in Brazil and soon was healing hundreds daily. None but drunkards were told to return tomorrow when sober.

Arigo began his short life in Brazil and by the sixties was healing unheard of numbers of afflicted ones, even hundreds daily. Arigo said an entity, a spirit presence calling itself Dr. Fritz had taken him over. We call it an incorporation by Arigo of the Doctor Fritz entity.

So when entranced, as he was constantly while healing, the entity not only guided his hand, but also dictated the various common herbs and drugs and how to use them, for each person.

Arigo had almost accidentally done his first healing of a prominent official, and Arigo, being in full trance, so remembering nothing, had gone in the room of this man which adjoined his in a hotel, and had healed him.

This was in 1950, ten years before he began full time healing. My friend Andreija Puharich had done major work in defense of Arigo, who was constantly harassed by the police. The healer said the spirit or entity who had taken him over had said that he was a military German doctor, calling himself Dr. Fritz, who had died in 1918.

I said in my chapter on the Healing Buddha, Rinpoche had his start as an esperitista priest in Brazil. He told me that many self-styled healers, who claimed to have inherited Dr. Fritz guides, were deluded.

In 1971, Arigo died in a car wreck. Puharich thought that other similar healers would continue to arise. This, as I had written on genius, would not be possible.

And now on to Joao of God, who in his early days was an ordinary school boy. He began to have times when he had states of trance and spoke to others prophetically. The only book about Joao seems to be that of R.P. Estrich, *The Miracle Man*. It lacks dates, etc., so I ask my readers to accept the scenario I present:

At about age sixteen, he started to heal people who sought him out. In the next twenty years he endured agonies equivalent to the dark night of the soul of St. John, with profound trances and slow perfection of his art of healer. Later he suffered harassment and many beatings by the police. By the seventies, or possibly years earlier, a facility was built in Abadihnia, where he is today.

This sounds like a poor description of Arigo's way—but not true. I must here tell you by what I saw and felt and know from my visit to Joao, and his healings of me—now in their earliest stages.

Joao conveys his powers through what he calls "surgeries". These only are external, and therefore visible, in persons under 53. In my old carcass of 87, all surgeries are invisible and done only through the mind of Joao by contact and invasion of my mind. I become accessible to Joao's entities and willingly and gratefully incorporate them at the deepest levels of my psyche.

Joao says he works with as many as thirty or more of these discarnates (spirits now they are dead). Following each mental and personal surgery contact, one feels totally wiped out and needs complete rest for 24 hours.

There are many accessories to this process, such as: sermons by his associates, guidance by other mediums, continuous meditation and prayers by scores of supplicants right in the same room and neighboring rooms, all close to yours. These are all 'partners' in one's incorporation of particular entities suited to one's age, mental set, illnesses, etc.

One is from then on guided and his entities manifest in various ways, in my case via vivid lucid dreams suited to shake my psyche alive as to who is really in charge—not me—but Joao and his entities. Two or three times these came to me, in days or weeks at intervals since. They are easily recognizable as utterly foreign to any of my usual dreams (throughout 30 years of dream work with all varieties of experts from Freud to Jung, and beyond). These dreams are so chaotic and chthonic, as if to remind me who—what is actually in charge, and to my surrender to their ministrations so they can help me.

In a recent invasion by these rare and horrid dreams: I am in a dark building, all inside semi-dark—walls all around me are crumbling—wire cables cut off—burned off everywhere carrying forces all their own with total disarray—junk all over. But the whole is somehow merciful and merciless all at once, mid all the roaring chaos symbolic of the inner purification and cleansing, necessary and at all times at work toward my healing.

All this change may take weeks to months. It's a very slow process, totally different from the slash seeming brutal and immediate healings of Arigo who was the only one in trance asking no one else to be in trance as well.

I already feel some changes bodily but must be patient, for I am told my entities will tell me when and if I must return for other surgeries.

Venerable Segyu Choepel Rinpoche: The Healing Buddha

A pleasant meeting with my ever smiling friend. All these happy years of knowing him. Quick of mind, open hearted, replete with spiritual goings on. There is never a dull moment to be endured with this soldier of the glorious now and I always leave him feeling better about my life, even boring as it is at times.

He considers the relationship of the Guru and his devotee to be an eternal bond and is now involved with Lama Segyu Choepel Rinpoche, who was originally trained as a curandero or shaman in the espiritista tradition. Venerable Segyu Choepel Rinpoche is the founding director and head Lama of the Healing Buddha Foundation-Segyu Gaden Dhargye Ling. In 1985, the 98th Gaden Tri Rinpoche, Venerable Jampal Shenpen, Holder of the Gelugpa lieage founded by Lama Tsogkhapa, identified him as the reincarnation of Dorje Zangpo. In a ceremony held by the Segyu Monastery in Kathmandu, Nepal, on February 19, 1997, Venerable Segyu Rinpoche was formally recognized as the tulku (reincarnation) of venerable Gyudchen Dorje Zangpo the 16th century Tantric master of the Segyu lineage.

The Healing Buddha Foundation—Segyu Gaden Dhargye Ling—is dedicated to the dissemination of the Buddhadharma and was established in 1985 by Venerable Segyu Choepel Rinpoche to promote the study and practice of Tibetan Buddhism as taught within the Gelugpa Lineage and the Sed-Gyued Datsan Tantric College.

The Sed-Gyued Lineage of the Gelug School of Tibetan Buddhism is an unbroken line of tantric teachings descending directly from Lama Je Tsongkhapa (1357-1419), founder of the Gelug School.

Unique to the Healing Buddha Foundation are its Psycho-Spiritual Healing Clinics which address our culture's need for a healing therapy that considers a person's physical, emotional, and spiritual aspects. Techniques used in the clinics are based on Buddhist psychology and Tibetan Tantric Medicine.

One day when Rinpoche was practicing as a curandero in Brazil, a friend from his parish gave him a small statue of a saint. He came to have a strong attraction to this object, probably because it closely resembled a figure in a dream that he had when he was a younger man in which he felt protected by a hovering guardian. This Indian (Hindu) or Tibetan-looking holy man whom he frequently saw in his dreams, continued to watch over and guide him for many years.

He feels that this dream figure ignited his intense search for his spiritual way very early in his life. He kept that statue with him for years. One day his espiritista Guru picked it up and immediately fell into a profound trance state. While so entranced, he told Rinpoche that the Statue was of great value to him personally, and that he should always keep it close to himself, that it was the likeness of a Tibetan who had lived hundreds of years before, and who was the head of a healing order.

He said that this Tibetan healer was, in fact, his direct progenitor and that Rinpoche should seek out the Tibetans to the north (in the United States). Eventually, Segyu Choepel Rinpoche visited America and established relationships within the community of Tibetan Buddhist practitioners where he lived. It was their conclusion that he was the reincarnation of that same ancient Tibetan healing Lama, a tulku. After this he was initiated as the head of the healing order, a position which he still holds.

During his years of training as a Kardec practitioner, he was blessed to find an espiritista teacher whom he held in very high regard. Soon he became an outstanding practitioner, finding that he had a natural ability for healing the sick and mentally disturbed or possessed ones. His help and guidance were sought by many.

The only other substantial body of espiritista healers are the ones who are alive and well in the Philippines and others in Brazil. Tony Agpoa, a Philippine curandero, spoke to me about his early training and revealed that part of his development included the discipline of setting fires at a distance by mental means alone.

Greg Shulkin, an American espiritista healer, described the development of a facility whereby the healer's hands became independent of their mind and will, performing their own instinctual work. But Greg did not complete his studies and never attained this degree of skill, by his own confession. He regrets this, but just as Harry Roberts did, he chose our Western way in the end.

I have known Rinpoche for two years and I have asked for his help in healing several of my friends. I requested a distant healing of one of my fellow devotees here with metastatic cancer of the cervix. I attended two healing ceremonies on her behalf, each lasting several hours. The complex ritual was of great interest to me because it was a magical mixture of the Lama's Brazilian background combined with Tibetan Buddhist practices. The whole ritual was full of melodious chants and South American dancing. My friend did recover from her cancer and is still doing well today.

Another friend, his wife and his daughter were also helped by Rinpoche more recently. After just two sessions, Jim declared that he felt like a new man. I believe his trouble was primarily a spiritual one. I have known him for about twenty-five years. I also knew his wife before she suffered from schizophrenia. Jim felt most of the burden of responsibility for their daughter because his wife was non compos mentis so much of the time. He is a very sensitive man. Both he and his daughter were suffering from feelings of alienation and separation and felt like they were going off the deep end. They couldn't find any reason in their lives for this increased level of disturbance.

Jim told me that on his second appointment with Rinpoche he was confused about the time and arrived about an hour early. When Jim was announced for his appointment, the Rinpoche insisted that he was right on time and that he should be sent right in. The Rinpoche was in the center of a circle of devotees who were holding ribbons and dancing around him. At the climax of this ceremony, there was a loud explosion and the Lama seemed to be hurled through the air, landing in the arms of a large devotee. After this, Jim felt more securely present in his body—more than he had felt for weeks. His wife and daughter, who had been having symptoms of schizophrenia, no longer felt disturbed.

In my opinion, this exorcism proved to be far more effective for Jim and his family than the conventional therapeutic use of drugs and psychotherapy would have been. The espiritista tradition views most healing as a form of exorcism of evil spirits, or unhappiness. With such an attitude, they get a lot more "cures" than we do with conventional psychiatric care.

That is why spontaneous Kundalini arousals which are problematic are perhaps better treated by an exorcist than a therapist. When the negative features of this arousal appear to be disturbing or destructive, this can lead to a rather desperate state. The other alternative is to practice in the company of a real Guru. Those whose Kundalini is aroused by a real Guru don't seem to have these kinds of complications.

Gabriel Cousens made a similar observation in his work at the Muktananda Ashram in New York. When people experience the arousal of the Kundalini in the company of a genuine Spiritual Adept and a community that understands what is going on, they have a much easier time with it.

It seems to me that there are certain kinds of attitudes and beliefs that positively influence the outcome of this kind of healing work. I have noticed that there is a corresponding openness to a miraculous outcome in the people who have received the greatest benefit. And most of these willing souls had accepted the idea of reincarnation as well. And if one has also accepted the idea that we choose our parents to learn a particular lesson in this life, then we can hardly blame them for helping us to learn. It throws the whole show on our own shoulders where it mostly belongs.

In my extensive work with schizophrenics I found that certain of the symptoms seemed to have a connection with the presence of forces that the medical descriptions of schizophrenia did not encompass. They also gave me the feeling that I was dealing with forces from the primordial and aboriginal world views. The aboriginals made the whole of their lives a connection with spirits quite unknown and unacceptable to our psychiatric studies.

These spirit forces could not be included in the psychiatric view of mental illness. It is beyond the limits of our cultural discourse. And in order to address these phantoms, you would really need to embrace another language, an aboriginal language, which is far more than most Western medical practitioners are capable of. It's an endeavor which is more vast and complex than any one man or priest or sect or group of ambitious writers can deal with.

Early in my practice I assiduously avoided the negative magical aspects (black magic) of my disturbed patient's process. But after many years of witnessing bilocation, teleportation, psychokinesis and other supernatural phenomenon, I became willing

to become more curious about those areas that our cultural taboos had rendered invisible.

I use Jim's case as an example. It's another miracle of healing, of the actual dimensions of genius in people's minds and hearts and bodies which have been defeated time after time by the forces of resistance. It is just awe inspiring to think of the limitations that most of us are born with as far as our thinking, and our psyche, and our healing of ourselves and others is concerned. All you can do is stand in awe of anyone who is effectively dealing in these areas.

My friend was privileged to accompany Rinpoche into the far reaches of the Sierras recently on a complex and challenging mission. They went into the Sierras on skis to a remote region which has been set aside for unregenerate souls—souls who have never come to terms with their own evil natures. These are the real baddies and those who must remain on the subtle level.

But there are some who are trained to evoke them and work with them, trying to improve their karmas very slowly. It takes a whole tradition to do this. A whole generation of priests. They evidently find that it infinitely increases their own resources to deal with more complex karmas and real evil.

I am struck with appreciation for these cultural reservoirs of great depth and their wisdom-filled observation of the progressions of karma. This form of service to wayward souls is a cultural and historical obligation to them. This kind of obligation must be inconceivable to most modern people as we blithely pursue our small and dull lives of equally small and limited scope, not having the traditional context which fosters this type of skill in the subtle realms.

I felt that I was in the presence of the hallowed when I was being told about this process. And I believe this is a matter which should provoke a whole overturning of our cultural values, how we experience evil and what, if anything we do about it. This right orientation to human karmic patterning and the skills required to negotiate more dangerous subtle forces may be intimately linked with our own ultimate survival here on earth.

On the Guru

In an odd way, my search for the Divine is intimately connected with a sense I have of the ridiculousness of man at his egoic best. Every few years, through one fortunate maneuver or another (all quite illogical, spontaneous and haphazard), I am able to enter that joyous domain, the dimension that dwarfs all others, in which I know for certain that I am, that I was, and that I will be, again and again. By now, I know that the enlightened state in any permanent sense is beyond me in this life. I also know that in these dreadful times of the "Kali Yuga," the devotional impulse in Western man is very dim and waning probably faster than waxing.

Even so, the depth of my bond with various teachers and gurus I have encountered is more often manifest than I had any right to hope for. It is part and parcel of that more profound and gigantic dimension of which I have often spoken.

Via a relationship to a true teacher or guru, some of us possess the potential for touching real joy, hope and truth here and now. To have a guru entails surrender since to do disciplines for their own sake is useless. The guru's "transmission" necessitates the capacity of the devotee to form a very deep psychic link. Ordinary people have this capacity to benefit from the influence of one who is wiser, more experienced, knowledgeable and masterful in these trance or samadhi states, in short, an enlightened being such as I have found in my guru, Adi Da Samraj.

Ordinary psychic linking, or communication between persons who are otherwise quite "normal" is not usually dignified by the august label of "transmission". Transmission is used in speaking of communication between a devotee and his or her guru and seems to have similar features whether experienced during "sighting" the guru in person or during meditation. In both cases, I notice a kind of calm, with very little interference by my mind's wandering thoughts, and I sink into a deeper silence and stillness of mind. In the midst of this, I become aware of a pressure deep in the center of my forehead, which, when I am able to focus more deeply, begins to increase and then to lessen as I am able to relax further and lose all sense of my body.

When a devotee can surrender, relinquishing all attention, the Guru is able to "appear" in the devotee's inner landscape. I become unusually psychic during these focused times. There is an immense feeling of being immersed in the Guru's unmistakable Presence, overwhelming my entire consciousness, so powerful that, at times, it becomes impossible for me to bear it—and I blast right back into my little conscious world. These experiences attest to the potential of a guru both to serve the meditative process and to draw the devotee beyond the egoic territories with which he is habitually associated.

For instance, if people who have kundalini experiences are without the support of a spiritual teacher and other grounding influences—even if these experiences are largely positive—they will likely become boring and not of any real use. This bodily-based energy is self-generated, and it can take place outside the context of relationship with others. In my experience, more often than not, people soon grow impatient with all of these displays if they occur outside the context of a spiritual practice.

The relationship between a guru and a devotee is a special one and not much valued in our fragmented culture today. While this role is a talent and gift which is rarely discussed here, there is still a very well preserved tradition in India, for example, in which such a relationship is greatly valued.

The great ones—gurus, saints, prophets, realizers— each represent the most Divine possibilities of mankind. I have had more "real" gurus and spiritual practices than I can count on all my fingers and toes: Muktananda, Suzuki Roshi, Krishnamurti (UG), Tarthang Tulku, Trungpa Rinpoche, de Ropp, Subud, Daddy Bray, Elsie Parrish, Eknath Easwaran, Baker Roshi, Dr. Seo, Sister Denise, Maezumi Roshi, etc., but I couldn't surrender enough to any to receive and truly benefit from them. It was only in the company of Adi Da Samraj that I realized the truth of the statement that "the Guru will do everything if only the devotee will truly surrender and adhere to the Guru's instructions."

When one's focus enters this domain of continuous guru love, the meditative state drops into place suddenly. I, myself, became aware of a pleasurable pressure between the eyes—something different than I had ever felt before. It was like an energy field of intense force penetrating me to the exclusion of any other thing. It was benign but scary as hell. At times, I was overwhelmed by bliss and feelings of immense love. It was the beginning of a process which is mysterious and sure and wild, as is the nature of the guru.

As a psychiatrist with a wide spiritual background, I have been looked to as something of an authority on gurus— especially those mad ones in and out of the literature. But you see, anyone in the so-called higher stages of life cannot be judged by our usual reductive approaches, which hardly suffice for true understanding of even ordinary ones of us, regardless of our most refined psychological dissections. They (the great spiritual figures) cannot be linearly measured by our usual ego standards. Thus, the feeling approach is better but the deep psychic and spiritual approach is even superior.

Just turning to a guru does not suffice. In the words of Adi Da Samraj, "There must be a fundamental and profound sense of the nature of existence. The religious life takes place in the context of what you presume to be reality, i.e., if your presumptions of what surrounds you are mechanical and one dimensional, then that is the desert where you practice."

Recently, with my exploration of genius came a recognition of my own history of spiritual searches. The two subjects suddenly became relevant to each other and demonstrated to me a congruence which had previously gone unnoticed and unexamined. I believe that most gurus are geniuses. Does devotion and submission to a realized guru serve the devotee in finding their own genius? In my observation, a guru makes manifest the divinity of the devotee and in the process ignites the divine spark of genius within that devotee.

In Adida's latest edition of *The Love-Ananda Gita*, the introduction has several pages on what he means by turning to him completely and forgetting oneself by:

> ...invoking him with the mind, the feeling and emotions, the physical body, the breath, and through service. Included is an admonition that comes to us through the tradition of Jesus and the *Hebrew Bible* or *Torah* which instructs us to turn to or love the divine via each of the four principle faculties.

A TRADITIONAL ADMONITION TO TURN THE ENTIRE BEING TO THE DIVINE

From *The Da Love-Ananda Gita—The Free Avataric Gift of The DivineLove-Bliss*

by The Ruchira Avatar, Adi Da Samraj

In the introduction to this section, Jonathan Condit Ph.D writes:

"Throughout history, serious religious and Spiritual practitioners have been naturally and spontaneously moved to turn to the Divine with the entire being. The following well-known saying attributed to Jesus of Nazareth (which is based on similar admonitions from the *Hebrew Bible*) can, in fact, be understood as instruction to turn to (or "love") the Divine via each of the four principal faculties:

And thou shalt love the Lord thy God

with all thy heart,
and with all thy soul,
and with all thy mind,
and with all they strength.

This is the first commandment.

Mark 12:30"

Adi Da has used the following terminology in expressing this admonition:

Heart: the faculty of emotion
Soul: the faculty of breath
Mind: the faculty of mind
Strength: the faculty of body

(The English "soul" is a translation of Greek "psyche"—a word that originates from the Greek verb "psychein", meaning to breathe.")

A remarkable piece of research by a Jewish scholar, Israel Knohl, was published in 2000 by the University of California Press, titled *The Messiah Before Jesus—The Suffering Servant of the Dead Sea Scrolls*. The hero of this book on an earlier messiah shows how Christianity emerged from Judaism. Jesus was born after the life time of this earlier messiah, inheriting the mantle of "the suffering servant" of the Dead Sea Scrolls from the earlier "Jesus" of Biblical lore.

I have added this research as an example of my original thesis—that genius is a continuous and irrepressible characteristic of mankind which arises out of man's creative and always-present urge to contribute to the general welfare of his fellow beings.

In the *New York Times,* Friday, September 9th, 2005, an article reported on a challenge to ideas that human evolution essentially stopped fifty thousand years ago. The new finding by Bruce T. Lahn and colleagues of the University of Chicago led to the "surprising suggestion that the brain is still undergoing rapid evolution." It is good to see that science now may support examples given in several of these chapters ascertaining the evolution of genius.

A Summing Up
Featuring William Blake

I have not forgotten the geniuses in all forms of the arts, the geniuses who make our very lives worth living. Instead I have focused on the geniuses who have become victimized by their societies and become our endangered species, the geniuses who had and still have the potential to truly change our lives and ensure that humankind has a planet which can provide the proper continuation of human existence.

We have looked back and seen the toll that has been taken:

Some like Bentov become distracted. Just before he died he told me, "Lee, I can't do the research that cries to be done."

Adam Trombly was three times on the verge of developing free energy from the vacuum of space. After several betrayals by high government sources here, he is hopefully alive and hopefully well.

George Page was grossly betrayed at every turn and his precious crystals disappeared from his life's wreckage at the end. His optical glass could have revolutionized all quartz glass applications, perhaps with telescopes ten times as powerful as the present ones.

And what of Nikola Tesla? Consider what undreamed-of possibilities could have been realized if we had known how we could get endless power from Earth or even from cosmic sources and not need oil (and all other power sources) as our primary source of energy. But Westinghouse looked at this possibility Tesla had shown him and he is quoted as moaning and saying, "But what of my Anaconda Copper investments?" and immediately withdrew all support to Tesla. And that was only a small part of Tesla's miracles yet undisclosed and which never will be, now that he is no more.

If only a few of these I have written about had been not only allowed to realize their genius, but also had been properly protected, promoted and encouraged, we could now have: Naessens' understanding of biology which would have revolutionized all organ transplantation (made free and easy); Royal Rife's cancer cure; Arigo's cure for all other body-mind disorders. The list of possibilities is endless.

By the time I had contacted most of these "modern" geniuses, they had not failed; they produced all of the hardware and signs of the essences of which they had spoken. But to their and our disappointment could not give it away—not because of the intent to get revenge on the world but because they have lost contact.

They all dreamed they could, by an effort of will, be reconnected—no way—they had not the wits to tell us the way or what they had known and now have lost. Most of them have died with their illusions intact—thinking that at this late date they could still DO.

But their societies did not allow them to DO. One of our great lessons to keep in mind is that we must remember that genius is fragile. Henry Miller said, "The task of genius, and humanity is nothing if not genius, is to keep the miracle alive, to live always in the miracle, to make the miracle more and more miraculous, to swear allegiance to nothing, but live only miraculously, think only miraculously, die miraculously." The geniuses, passionate pioneers, who were destroyed lived in societies which had no grasp of this miracle, societies which undid them.

It seems that not only our leaders but also much of our population is fatally attracted to one of the easiest to come by and most deadly sins of all: raw, unmitigated greed for wealth and power. This atmosphere of the present time has pervaded generation after generation and has allowed this deliberate and disastrous destruction of genius after genius. In doing so our world has been denied its possible salvation. Imagine the potential which has been and is still being crushed because of being destroyed by miserable war-driven and power-hungry paranoids who wipe them out if they are seen as getting in their way. Their destruction not only denies the world of a way to change our lives into true visions of a new Golden Age, but also puts our planet into jeopardy.

(It is important to note here how dangerous it can be to be a genius, dangerous not to the body but to the soul. The power/greed carrot has tragically been used to encourage and exploit geniuses who somehow have become devoid of the jewel of humankind, a conscience, making them donkeys pursuing the carrot, corrupting their genius by channeling it into the production of such horrors as nuclear bombs, germ warfare, poisonous gas, the notorious gas ovens and the continued rape of the planet.)

We who have less obvious genius must contribute our bit, in any way we can. With this book, I am trying to do this, never ceasing my search for and the encouragement of geniuses and sharing with them the utter fragility of genius itself, knowing it must be continuously attended to until its realization.*

I did not intend to discuss geniuses in the arts until a friend introduced me to the great English poet William Blake as the one genius in art and literature I needed to read and study and admire. He was so right! It takes our poets, not our scientists to express more clearly and deeply what we need to know about genius. The truths Blake wrote of in Jerusalem about 200 years ago have barely been considered today. He addressed the killers of the dream thusly: *Go tell them that the worship of God is honoring His gifts in other men (people) and loving the greatest best, each according to his genius which is the Holy Ghost in man: there is no other god than that God who is the intellectual fountain of humanity.*

note: Youngsters on the edge of fulfillment, often are without the thoughtful support of parents who are obviously loving—but without sufficient understanding of how fragile their child's state is. Without intent to do harm, they often exploit their small charges. Thus prodigies tend to burn out.

This is the statement of genius that was in everything he touched, his undying lithographs and in every word he wrote. This connectedness of God = GENIUS burst on this world with hardly any attention paid to it. He was laughed at as inept, a fool. "A prophet is not without honor except in his own country." Blake spoke of The Divine as The Original Poetic Genius all of his creative life, as did his fellow genius Ludwig Von Beethoven who died in the same year, passing from this earth glorifying the angels, and singing joyfully at the sight of them as they approached.

Over hundreds of thousands of years, steadily and relentlessly, the geniuses from stone-age cultures to ours have left their imprints. Only genius, from its first appearance in hominoids, was ever that force which drove mankind on and up. In truth, it is *only* by genius that mankind can continue to evolve by stopping our headlong rush into hell (heading toward our own Kali Yuga), only genius which can allow humankind to pursue a golden age instead, moving on even to the stars. Is this possible?

It is spoken, that if we are destroyed, there will be our inevitable rebirth, the glory that the Master of All and All assures us of, by his gifts without end. The promise is that these natural progressions will continue and will prevail — driven by genius however long it takes. The Divine will always provide the spark. You and I and the world must do the fulfillment ourselves.

Remind yourself always, *Do not do what you hate.* What do I love? can become a mantra or even a prayer for this great change possible in every being in this lifetime. I repeat: the Divine Essence gives each of us some spark of Genius which, if not exercised, will never be presented again.

If we can know our own genius on earth, the better chance toward its completion in our prayer to the Great One and the greater is our thanksgiving for this great gift of knowing. Whatever our next lesson we are presented with in this great school, the sooner we know what our genius is, the sooner we can advance toward its mysterious completion. Our genius, when fulfilled and realized, will be the measure of how we have paid our debt to the Divine, or how we have fulfilled our task to make and acknowledge our contact with the Divine by manifesting our own genius, which process is called prayer. In this way we will have accelerated our job of consciousness and taken the next step towards perfection.

Now if we look at genius deeply, we will eventually come to the subject of eternal return or reincarnation. We will find the proper teachers as guides to move us to our next task in the astral realm. I assume we will judge ourselves in accordance with how clear we are about our heart's desire. What is likely is that we will continue returning, in the end, till each of us comes to his or her own essence of being, and then joins the heavenly hierarchy.

About the Author

My father and mother lived in Boston where my father was a student at Tufts Medical School. Just before I was born my mother returned to Springfield to live with her parents and await my birth. I was born in May, 1916, and soon after my father was graduated. We all lived with my grandparents, while my father interned in Springfield Hospital and where my sister was born and until my father opened his own office for the practice of medicine.

My sister and I were raised without any influence of organized religion. There were no proscriptions as far as voicing ideas, choice of books or experiences. I became an Eagle Scout but also played violin and guitar in a band in a raunchy nightclub. Music became my goal and I set my sights on being a professional composer. But reality set in and I abandoned the thought. Having a doctor for a father and going on house calls with him probably helped me in pursuing a career in medicine. The choice felt good, right, natural, almost ordained.

After High School I spent two years at American International College in Springfield, the same school my father attended. The high points of those years were playing on the soccer team, tennis team and other exploitations of my vital physical self (including girls).

However, I transferred in my third year to Massachusetts State College (later the University of Massachusetts), planning to get into the best medical school I could think of. At the end of that term, I was interviewed at Yale (THE school) where they accepted me on the spot. I had a wonderful four years of medicine with princes and princesses for professors whom I loved dearly.

174

My first religious experience happened while I was in Medical School in my second year. I remember sitting at my desk and studying and all of a sudden I felt I was in a different space and I just experienced this flow of knowledge and intuition of every function of my body. I knew its physiology, its chemistry, how it worked, what it was for as a unity. I could scan my whole body and review it with an intimate understanding. It was what I would call a unity experience.

I was left with this beatific vision of the body, its physical and chemical processes and sensitivities. It was like the climax of a love affair with my own physiology and all that I had been stuffing myself with in medical school. Everything that I had been studying took its place in a Gestalt that was more than a sum of its parts, it had a religious dimension which I would later recognize more literally as the Divine. It was simply a prelude to that without any great to-do. It was sort of like an admission at the physical level that I was in love with what I was studying. I was overwhelmed by its beauty, its completeness. It became infused with meaning for the first time.

One of my first interests in medical research arose in my fourth year of medical school. My resulting paper was published in the Yale Journal of Biology and Medicine in the same year.

Just about this same time, before graduating, I contracted an infantile form of tuberculosis. Immediately I went home for enforced bed rest. While there I read omnivorously and listened to album after album of all kinds of music. Yale never exacted any more course work from me and I was graduated in 1940, in the top third of my class.

Massachusetts Eye and Ear Infirmary in Boston acted on my application as a resident in ophthalmology and I secured that prime position. Because of the nature of my illness, I moved to a gentler climate and settled on the West Coast in the San Francisco area.

In order to complete my compulsory number of hours of eye-work, I associated with a doctor in Reno and had a private practice for two years. I did a stint of ophthalmology as an itinerant physician, working from a trailer in which my wife and I lived and from which I practiced as I roved through sparsely-settled rural areas in Nevada.

In the mid-fifties I had been struggling for fifteen years with the white plague I hasd contracted in medical school. During that time I had more than one near death experience before the active infection finally succumbed to the newly developed streptomycin. Unfortunately, the antibiotic dosage left me with permanent vestibular damage.

Also in 1955 I became board certified as an ophthalmologist. In 1957 and again in 1959 I was asked to become a Board Examiner. This is an honor unheard of for someone without a formal residency in ophthalmology. I accepted in 1957 but didn't accept the second time because I felt that I had already disqualified myself by my other interest, Psychiatry. I had concentrated on ophthalmology as the most efficient way to earn a living and which would give me time enough to devote myself to the eventual practice of psychiatry but I didn't choose to take my boards in that field. This worked well. I practiced Ophthalmology privately and continued my psychiatric training program as a resident physician in Psychiatry at Napa State Hospital.

I was also active in other programs, in training programs at UC, acting as controller for the University students in training in clinical psychology and in full-time training myself. Continuing my research I took an opportunity that was offered to experience a single set of CO_2 inhalations. The complexity of results enhanced my understand of what this kind of treatment could effect.

There was a dramatic session in Napa in which I was training the resident physician in charge of the Substance Abuse program. He was in the process of rehabilitating some severe alcoholics. I was in charge of a session in which I administered Carbogen. My patient was an ex Navy man. Among the gathering were a number of candidates, some of whom I had already given CO_2 to, and others who awaited their sessions.

I started the gas inhalation and soon noticed that this obviously angry man who had furiously come into the room was about to give us trouble. I turned to the group and asked for their help. I had already warned them that I might need assistance when they were coming out of the coma. I turned to them and said: "Four of you quickly surround this man and restrain him."

This seething ex-soldier then nearly threw all four of the men against the wall so I called for more men to come and help. Then, as several men held him he faced me and violently spat at me, proceeding to tell me in detail how he would kill me when he got loose of these restraining fellow inmates. I let him continue.

Then, at one point I suddenly moved up to within a few inches of his face, gaining his attention and said: "What about your father?" And he stopped dead in his tirade against me and stared at me as if he were seeing a ghost or some such horror. Then he burst into tears.

As he sobbed, I put my hands on him and told the men holding him: "He's OK now. Let him go." Then he quieted down and told us that he had experienced a terrible memory, never before available, of his father being pulled under a tractor and killed right before his eyes when he was two years old. A bit more back and forth occurred and this session was over. The man was obviously free of his hatred of the world and all of us who had done this awful thing of depriving him of his father at such a vulnerable age when he was too young to help himself. He walked out of the room relaxed and smiling.

Years later I became somewhat of an expert in assisting people who had unpleasant or even disabling flashbacks as the result of material emerging that was not sufficiently worked through after their originally negative experiences with pot or LSD.

I was in charge of the most disturbed adolescents who were hospitalized in the psychiatric ward there. I was to replace a doctor who would be away for six weeks. He left word that I was to employ any kind of therapeutic modality that I wished.

Naturally, I first asked to do LSD work—which of course (as I wrote earlier) was refused. These were the days when LSD became highly illegal for use in any but the most highly placed university teams under government supervision.

Before they clamped down on it, it had been used by daring experimenters, both medical and non-medical. It was one among many other drugs such as Ketalar which was used as an anesthetic for children—roundly abused in its overuse—after all what child is going to report the bizarre visual and sensory alterations that such an agent promoted regularly. Ketalar was also finally proscribed and became available only for veterinary medicine. This same story goes on today with such relatively minor mind altering agents as marijuana which, after all, was perfectly legal 100 years ago and was widely used in medicine. Like Carbogen, it can be useful to reveal data about the unconscious which is very valuable for investigative research in one of the outstanding plagues, schizophrenia. It is throwing the baby out with the bath-water to ban such drugs from adequately controlled, humanly approached research.

So, instead of administering that controversial hallucinogen, LSD, I resorted to a more customary diversion. I got the go ahead on alcohol. Only the most difficult patients were given some orange juice and vodka. The first one on my list was a non-responsive nine year old "head-banger". He had a well-deserved reputation for attempting to pulverize any unwary child who approached his bed. He had been in restraints for a while. When I came to his bedside, I could see that he was obviously quite inebriated. I came closer, wary of his explosive violence, but instead he did something that no one had seen him do before. He simply smiled happily and tried to reach up to me with his hands. I asked the attendants to remove his upper body restraints. He continued to relate to me, and then to a child nearby as well, in a friendly manner. Then I asked for the removal of all the other straps and he began his first day of free interaction with the others, He was a new being when drunk, and completely tractable.

I went on to open my own psychiatric clinic in Berkeley in 1962 and ran it until 1972. There I conducted gatherings of self-selected, regular patients. Through my continued interest in research, I worked with them and together we tested little-known ways to forward more effective and humane psychiatric treatments including using LSD and carbogen inhalations. This was the earliest of the self-help, lay-trained and led assistance programs and it became a model for other professionals. I was gratified when the AMA Psychiatric Association asked me to write an article on the training of laymen to engage my style of group and single-patient practices.

I also ran an in-patient service for substance abuse problems in a rented house in Berkeley. We provided group therapy several times a week since this type of problem cannot be managed over the long-term with private visits alone. We found that group therapy with a buddy system gave us the best results.

One of the women in these groups had been labeled schizophrenic. She had made serious attempts at suicide and only could function well after a session with carbon dioxide inhalation therapy. These treatments had a beneficial effect on her for only a few hours or at most half a day.

Several years later, after she had moved to the northwest, someone prescribed Lithium for her and it had a profoundly restorative effect. After a few days of taking this prescription, she looked out of her kitchen window one morning and noticed, for the first time, that there were flowers on the lawn. It seems that she had been suffering a loss of color vision which was functional in nature and that her schizophrenic defense was her response to a bi-polar disorder.

She steadily improved over the next few months. This was after twenty years of being labeled schizophrenic.

She became the village saint and later studied and became an ordained minister, a post which she still occupies.

Because of her, I have always advised a trial of Lithium on any schizoid or schizophrenic or psychotic patient as a simple screening method. It often works miracles. I also requested permission to administer a color vision screening test to psychotic patients at the Napa hospital, but I was summarily refused. I was curious about the coincidence. Unfortunately, that research was never undertaken.

Another fence, that I chose to be on the wrong side of, was the administration of electro-shock therapy, or EST. Early in my training as a resident, Dr. Carl Pribram, a famous neurologist, gave a pivotal lecture on EST. He stated categorically that he had examined brains three to five days after EST and in every case the brains exhibited inflammation and heavy bleeding from the severe damage caused by the so-called "therapy". I responded to this outrage by refusing to learn to give EST. And I never did. I only knew one colleague and friend who administered EST in a humane and merciful manner which was only in a circumstance when he felt that it might be lifesaving.

His judicious use of this modality and his utter humanity eliminated many of the worst side-effects. The travesty of its widespread use as a form of punishment is one of the darkest terrors of the hospitalized mentally ill. One patient came to me in utter desperation, afraid of losing what mind she had left. Her husband, and his brother who was a psychologist, had decided that she was 'too hard to handle'. The two of them convinced a psychiatrist to give her EST once a month to 'calm her down'. I saw this woman in consultation after she had suffered a stroke which had involved the visual cortex. I felt that her stroke was probably caused by the electro-shock treatment that had been administered a few days earlier. Her psychiatrist picked up on my negative feelings about EST and I assured him that he was correct. I warned him that to proceed would be extremely dangerous for her, if not fatal.

I was once attending a course which was offered by two male psychologists. One of the attendees, a friend of one the presenters, went into a mini-psychotic state as a result of the stress of the sessions, becoming completely unresponsive. I had left the room for a minute and returned to find these two well-meaning gentlemen in a state of near panic after realizing that they were incapable of dealing with her. Without a word, I immediately sat down on the floor beside her and got her attention. As she reached out to take my hands she almost immediately returned to the living, so to speak, and the meeting resumed with the two psychologists taking charge once more.

I consider myself very fortunate to have lost not even one person to suicide in my thirty-five years of psychiatric practice, even though I took on many psychotic and suicidal patients. Here I repeat the injunction that possession-like symptoms in those who are diagnosed as psychotic or those with schizophrenic-like states are probably more successfully helped by a capable priest or shaman than by all of the anti-psychotic drugs, psychotherapies and EST currently at the disposal of our Western psychiatrists.

My wonderful professors at Yale Medical School were so truly caring, so encouraging that it made it easy for me to pursue medicine beyond the physical. My comfort in this area was demonstrated in 1967 when my book on kundalini was published. My appreciation is now represented by a Yale Medical School scholarship in two names, mine and my father's. It favors a student who shows some evidence of the understanding and importance of the spiritual in the healing arts.

It was an important event for me: to attend my fiftieth reunion at Yale. I carried the image of my marvelous professors and the spirit they represented with me. However, it was clouded by the deeply disturbing appointment of the former head of the FDA as the new Dean of the Medical School. The unapologetic pursuit of pharmaceutical moneys has apparently left Yale's research program permanently flawed. For those who had developed respect for holistic medical practices, this appointment felt like a direct assault. We were all aware of this man's history of selectively prosecuting physicians who had embraced alternative therapies. As I spoke with the various professors and alumni there, it was hardly comforting to find several others who agreed that this appointment was a travesty and that it represented a tragic turning point in their alma mater's history. Would there now be room for students interested in researching the physiology of altered states? Perhaps there will be in order to keep up with other medical schools who go beyond the physical.

My medical research and my aspirations to do more had been abandoned as I became focused on my primary interest—the immortality of spirit. Now, later in my life, as I look back at my first religious experience in medical school, I would interpret its religious dimension as a glimpse of another psychic dimension. This intuition of Conscious-ness, of which I had been aware since my earliest childhood was simply more attractive to me than the possibility of doing further research in such far out animal and human physiology at this point in my life.

It is not surprising with the background I have, to have spent forty years trying to understand various states of consciousness in my own body-mind. This story is my attempt to portray the experiences, insights, experiments, conversations and loving exchanges which formed the shape and substance of that inquiry. In some instances, my query led to direct personal contact—at all levels of intensity, humor, and love—as apprentice, or even, as teacher. This whole realm—from material to cosmic—has become a means to search for consonance or vibrational equivalents. I am still searching, still following my passion.

Postscript

When my wife and Tresa and I moved to the West Coast, we joined the Society of Friends and were Quakers for over twenty years, our four children growing up in that religion. Even though Tresa and I are divorced, I still have a place, a second home, in the house we had built for us and where Tresa still lives. Our children and grandchildren are often there, enjoying returning to the nest and the swimming pool.

Both Tresa and I were in helping professions, Tresa a nurse and I a doctor. One of our daughters is a school teacher, one a scholar and professional harpist and one, an actress and a supporter of the arts, who is planning to teach. Although our son is in business, he has become an expert in the discipline of aikido. He and I have spoken about how it trains the body toward the spiritual dimension and possibly how it becomes part of one's genius, or a preordained aggregate early known and powerfully honed into all one's adult life.

I feel blessed to have such fine children, to see them developed into such admirable adults, and to see their beautiful offspring, my grandchildren and great-grandchildren.

One of the reasons for recording this part of my life is so that my children and Tresa may get a bit broader glimpse of me than was possible from my random and many times covert excursions (as a way of thinly disguising and, at the same time, revealing my almost desperate need to be heard by them) off into the blue, in almost drunken heedlessness of their feelings. It had to be confusing for the children as I veered away from my medical practice which they understood and took the path to the study of the spirit in which they were not able to participate or learn about. Added to that, after I was divorced and living away from Tresa's, physical distance further increased our lack of closeness.

They must have felt eons away from me, my activities seeming to them like just scramblings around. But not to me. These visions, ultimately, are the most precious values that I have tried to live by and with any luck, I will be graced to die by.

I hope after reading this book, they will feel that they will know me better, that they will see my vision, my passion and recognize its power in my life and theirs.